The Ultimate Book of Soccer Set-Pieces

For Tony Jr. and Carole Englund and Ted and Joan Anderson

TONY ENGLUND

THE ULTIMATE BOOK OF SOCCER SET-PIECES

STRATEGIES FOR ATTACK AND DEFENSE RESTARTS

Meyer & Meyer Sport

British Library of Cataloguing in Publication Data
A catalogue record for this book is available from the British Library

The Ultimate Book of Soccer Set-Pieces
Maidenhead: Meyer & Meyer Sport (UK) Ltd., 2022
ISBN: 978-1-78255-229-1

© 2022 by Meyer & Meyer Sport (UK) Ltd.
Aachen, Auckland, Beirut, Cairo, Cape Town, Dubai, Hägendorf, Hong Kong, Indianapolis,
Manila, Maidenhead, New Delhi, Singapore, Sydney, Tehran, Vienna
Member of the World Sport Publishers' Association (WSPA), www.w-s-p-a.org
Printed by Bookwire

ISBN: 978-1-78255-229-1
Email: info@m-m-sports.com
www.thesportspublisher.com

CONTENTS

ACKNOWLEDGMENTS

This book is a product of strange times. I began writing the manuscript over the holidays in 2019. By the time I write this note, in April of 2020, the world is a different place amidst the Coronavirus pandemic. Soccer has been utterly sidetracked as so many of us watch, dumbfounded, as thousands die. Indeed, I vacillate between thinking that soccer seems pretty trivial compared to all of the concerns about avoiding and surviving illness on the one hand, and being immensely grateful for the thousands of hours I have spent on the field with friends before all of this madness set in. It seems that if there is a lesson to draw from this era it is coming at too great a price.

That said, one of the gifts of writing and learning is that they are pursuits that help us think about better times and the importance of focusing on the positive, even when it's difficult to find at times. I have been a coach for thirty years now, and it has been a wonderful, steep learning curve with lots of colorful personalities, good friends and great memories along the way.

I want to thank Meyer & Meyer publishing for supporting this writing project. I had the pleasure of meeting publisher Martin Meyer and editor Liz Evans for the first time in person in Baltimore in January of this year, and I was thoroughly impressed with their passion for people, education, and books. I asked them for permission to pursue this project because I feel sure that set-piece education is a major hole in the coaching literature and teaching curricula, and this is a facet of the game that coaches instinctively know can be decisive in a team's success or failure.

Nathan Klonecki is both my good friend and the leader of St. Croix Soccer Club, and he continues to construct my duties to suit my eclectic coaching, writing, and reading interests. I am thankful for our many detailed soccer conversations, often in deserted parking lots after training. He has had a profound influence on my understanding of the game.

Percy Hoff, Sr. is one of my favorite coaching friends. He and I met when we roomed together at the USC's Master Coach course, and I learned a great deal about coaching and life from our conversations. We are not often in touch, but he remains in my thoughts and he is a valued friend and mentor.

John Pascarella, who co-wrote with me the two books preceding the current effort, is another important mentor and friend. John was my instructor for the Master Coach course, and subsequently was kind enough to spend considerable time talking soccer and writing with me. I miss our soccer talks and look forward to catching up with him whenever our schedules allow.

Lisa Boeser, my long-time friend and chiropractor, has been an enduring source of inspiration and healthful thinking. Her wicked sense of humor and driven pursuit of fitness—physical and otherwise—are admirable and make life better for everyone in her care.

Dr. Robert Stoy deserves mention here for the decades of care he has given me. I have been a difficult and high-maintenance patient along the way, and his relaxed, reassuring approach to medicine and life have been critical to my ability to enjoy and understand life as a cancer survivor.

Russ Schouweiler and Chris Garcia-Pratts, the head coaches at Luther College in Decorah, Iowa, are first-rate coaches and people. I had the good fortune to watch them both work with their college teams for several years, and their inspirational, driven personalities continue to color my understanding of what good coaching looks like.

Mike Huber, with whom I have coached numerous championship teams over the past five years, is one of my favorite people. His unfiltered sense of humor destroys my concentration all of the time and also reminds me that we're just coaching soccer.

My sister, Tonja Englund, is the Head Women's Basketball Coach at the University of Wisconsin-Eau Claire. A former National Coach of the Year, she is a model of coaching behavior in every sense: Driven, professional, whip-smart, and always trying to improve the experience for her players.

Joan and Ted Anderson, my wife Beth's parents, and to whom this book is dedicated, have been kind, thoughtful friends who welcomed me into their wonderful family. Joan passed away in the spring of 2019, and Beth and I miss her every day. Ted was a long-time coach and teacher, and his love for watching sports is evidence of a lifetime of enthusiastically and selflessly supporting others.

Jake and Tess Wilder are my step-children. Both are charismatic, good people and I am very proud to call them family.

In a similar vein, Paul and Mark Anderson (and Mark's wife Jane), my brothers-in-law, are great people who consistently, like their sister, look on the bright side of life. My thanks to them for tolerating their sister's reclusive husband.

Carole and Tony (Jr.) Englund, my parents, are my beacons in this uncertain time. It is very hard to reconcile not seeing them (due to the virus lockdown) with being good for my or their health. On the other hand, I certainly appreciate them even more in their absence, and I look forward to visiting them again when conditions permit. Thank you both, again, for everything along the way.

My wife Beth has supported my soccer wanderings and writings from our first days together more than a decade ago. Frankly, it's difficult for me to remember how I managed to enjoy coaching or anything else without her. What I do know is that I'm a much better person and coach with her in my life. Much is left unsaid with me, but I want to say here that I love her very much.

1 IMPACT: THE INFLUENCE OF SET-PIECES ON THE MODERN GAME

World Cup 2018 saw a record 66 goals scored from set-piece situations (42% of the 155 total goals scored), a remarkable and emphatic statement regarding the influence of set-pieces on the modern game.

In the English Premier League, the number of set-piece goals reached 246 in the 2018-2019 campaign, up 10% over the previous campaign, and part of an evident trend over the past decade.[i]

A fascinating, recent study of three seasons in the English Premier League determined that teams were more likely to score from set-pieces (1.8%) as compared with normal possessions (1.1%).[ii] That same study pointed out that teams significantly improved their overall goals for/goals against ratio by excelling at defending set-pieces, and those same teams often found survival in the Premier League, or demotion, was related to their success at set-pieces.[iii]

Still, the following two statements apply to many coaches and teams at all levels of the game.

1. Resources for coaches to learn about and refine set-piece training are scant and dated.

2. Coaches tend not to devote a lot of training time to set-piece preparation.

Why?

Let's quickly examine the nature and challenges of the dearth of preparation for set-piece success.

Very little in the way of guidance for coaches exists to help them prepare their teams to win the set-piece battle. The written literature on the subject is largely dated and thin, and coaching schools generally eschew any in-depth exploration of set-pieces. Indeed, I was told by an instructor that "the selection of set-piece plays and defending thereof are dependent upon level, personnel, and the coaches' preferences." True enough. However, the same is often said of systems of play, which most of us debate in detail in coaching courses. Set-pieces arguably influence the outcome of matches at a level commensurate with systems of play.

Coaches tend to follow one or both of these two patterns in set-piece preparation:

1. complex plays they witnessed in watching high-level matches, or

2. coaches like to just give general themes for set-pieces (e.g., serve the ball to the penalty spot on corner kicks and have some runners converge there).

The result is that players and coaches often devote very little time to set-piece rehearsal, as this becomes a fairly dry and sometimes frustrating component of practice. Indeed, set-pieces are often one of the last topics added to the training docket, fit in as a necessity shortly before matches begin.

Consider, then, that teams average roughly 20 attacking set-pieces (free and penalty kicks, corner kicks and throws in the front third).[iv] Add on to this the potential damage of defending an average of twenty more set-pieces. If the team could win the set-piece battle, scoring more goals from set-pieces than are allowed, and if the team could achieve an increased proficiency by finishing, for example, two set-pieces per match, what kind of dramatic impact would this have on results? One has to think that if coaches at every level consider the trends and potential impact, there will be much more set-piece preparation going forward.

This volume is intended to be a complete exploration of the potential of set-piece situations in modern soccer. The body of the work will be a detailed examination of set-piece considerations on both sides of the ball and hundreds of examples of the most effective plays, as well as how to defend those situations. This book will be the most expansive, thoughtful study ever completed on the subject. It is hoped that coaches of every level will want to have this resource available to help prepare their teams.

PROCESS: SET-PIECE SELECTION

If the evidence that set-pieces have a decisive influence on the game is clear, and that selecting plays and training to attack and defend these situations is a desirable, but often less than efficient investment of training time, what must coaches do to incorporate set-piece preparation as a challenging, necessary component of training?

Coaches must first think through the requirements of each set-piece. Let's consider, for example, how many players should be deployed near the goal to defend a corner kick? Should the team put players on the post(s) in those situations? Zonal or one-on-one, or a mix? What are the goalkeeper's responsibilities? How will the team defend a short corner option?

The sharp trend toward the use of analytics to examine productive preparation has dramatic potential to influence how teams prepare. Indeed, many of the most recent and surprising statistical conclusions, drawn from scientific papers, are included in the body of this book. Clearly, there are myriad considerations.

As was pointed out in the previous section, each coach will also need to balance their own preferences with other variables.

Some additional considerations for every set-piece include:

1. The abilities of their team. A team that fields a lot of tall, less-mobile players may want to play more zone.

2. Age/level of their team. Clearly, younger youth teams will have less complex schemes in every sense for dealing with set-pieces.

3. The proclivities of their opponents. If the opponent always runs short corner kick plays, special consideration might be required as to how to close down these plays.

4. Weather. For example, defending corner kicks in the rain and/or heavy wind tends to be troublesome.

5. Match conditions. For example, if the team is leading by a goal late and concedes a corner kick, perhaps it will be desirable to add more players to the defensive scheme in front of goal.

6. In the case of defending corners, what is the team's attitude regarding counter-attacking after the serve? Some teams will risk more and leave an extra player up high in the hope that they can punish the opponent with a fast counterattack after the kick is defended.

After contemplating these and other variables, coaches must then select the best scheme(s) for their teams for each set-piece situation.

If the process of selecting and particularly implementing and rehearsing set-pieces is typically undertreated and static, what additional steps can be taken to make refinement more engaging and efficient? Set-piece training can be incorporated, either in the flow of training matches, or in active isolation, as a component of exercises to make it more intense and realistic. Many examples of both types of training are included in the final portion of the book. In addition, one of the most challenging aspects of set-piece training is preparing players and teams for the mental demands of these situations. Accordingly, the book also includes a concluding chapter on the importance of designing training to replicate the demands of the match set-piece situation.

Taken together, this discussion has highlighted the complex nature of set-piece design and the challenges of effectively preparing the team for set-piece execution in match situations.

2 SET-PIECES

KICK-OFFS

Kick-offs tend to be among the most neglected of set-pieces with regard to preparation. Most teams are of one of two mindsets. Some coaches simply want to keep the ball away from their own goal. Consequently, the team is instructed to play the ball deep to a corner in the opposition's end of the field. This is a safe option, particularly at the youth level, where the dangers of mental lapses across the team in the opening moments of play or the return to play after a goal can be a concern. The concern here is an obvious one, in that the team is conceding possession with just a few touches of the ball.

Other coaches want to get their players a touch on the ball and get the ball circulating immediately on the kick-off. These teams tend to knock the ball around in their own half a bit, developing rhythm and getting the team's identity on the ball established. The danger here, of course, is that there can be a tendency to turn the ball over given that the game has just started or restarted, and the opponent can be free to press without much concern and with fresh legs.

Who trains their team to defend kick-offs? Interesting question, and the answer is likely very few. Does the team ease into the defending, more concerned with keeping the ball in front of them, or does the team fly into their opponent's end, trying to win the ball immediately? Either way, the discussion and mentality are very important to how the team approaches defending kick-offs.

ATTACKING CONSIDERATIONS

1. Does the team want to go forward immediately?

2. Does the team prefer to knock the ball around and get everyone involved?

3. Is there a reliable long-ball server who can put the ball in a dangerous space right away?

4. How many players should the team commit to an immediate attacking move?

5. Does the team have speedy player(s) who can perhaps surprise the opponent off of the start?

6. Is there a player, perhaps not a front-line player, on whom the team should depend to start the attack? For example, perhaps there is a dominant personality in the midfield that is the target of any early possession after a kick-off.

7. Does a particular opponent offer an opening for a specific kick-off play? For example, a team that immediately presses high may be vulnerable to an early long ball service.

8. Does the team need multiple options, perhaps one for the opening kick-off and one for subsequent kicks?

picture alliance/dpa | Sven Hoppe

Marco Reus of Borussia Dortmund prepares to kick off a Bundesliga match at Bayern Munich.

ATTACKING PLAYS

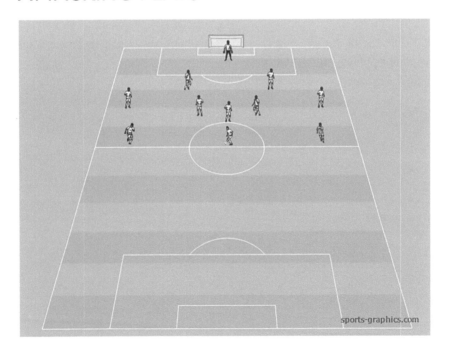

Typical attacking shape for a kick-off. Note the expanded shape, with the outside backs and wingers shading wider to create more space both for the attackers and also in the defensive shape of the opponent. Players likely to be involved in any opening move (i.e., the center forward and central midfielders) are arrayed around the ball. The center backs are split to give more room and better angles for possession, and the goalkeeper is in a position to be an outlet against early pressure. There are many variants, of course, but the general idea here is to give a framework from which players can be moved to create a particular attacking sequence.

Conservative Start

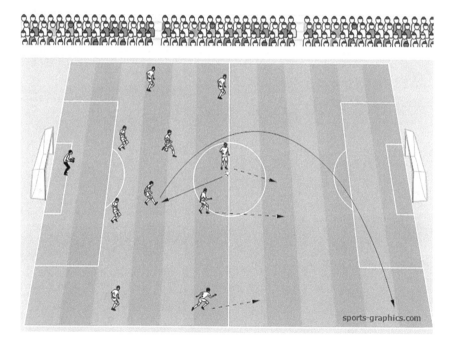

This is a safe option, and one that many coaches opt to pursue to start a game or half and also with a lead. Off of the kick-off, the striker plays a negative pass to a holding midfielder (this could be any player designated to play in that spot for the moment due to their ability to play a powerful long ball on a consistent basis). The holding midfielder plays the ball high and deep to a designated attacking corner of the field. It is very important that this ball be played deep enough to turn as many as possible of the opponents to face and move toward their own goal.

The coach can designate the level of pressure to be applied immediately to the ball. In the diagram above, the near-side wing, center forward and attacking midfielder begin to move toward the ball with the idea of applying pressure far from the team's goal. The coach might move the entire team forward, or opt to impose a *low restraining* line, perhaps allowing the other team to get into possession in with the idea that the team will be compact and able to defend against any long ball.

Flank Attack

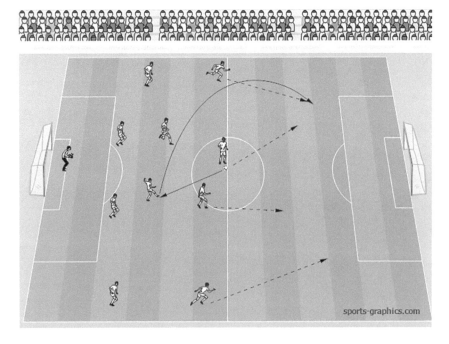

sports-graphics.com

This is a common approach to taking a positive, if low-risk, approach to the kick-off. Similar to the previous option, the ball is laid off and then played deep into the opponents' half. However, the target this time is not an area, but rather a winger. This approach can work well if the team possesses a dangerous, speedy player, who may win in an isolated duel with an unprepared or overmatched opponent. This approach is also recommended against teams who either press up high (caution the runner to stay on-side) or sit very deep (drop the ball in front of the back line). Note the supporting runs across the front line, as the winger will often need early assistance or want to quickly change the point of attack to one of the other runners.

Flank Overload

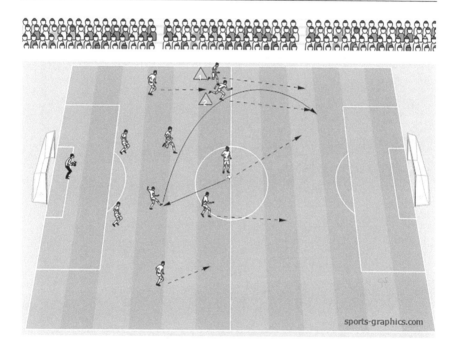

sports-graphics.com

This scheme builds on the idea of a flank attack and adds another runner, forming a target group. In the image above, the right-side winger has moved over to the left to join the left winger as targets for the midfielder's serve. Note also that the left back will follow-on in case the attackers need an immediate support option. Encourage the two wingers to think in advance how they will exploit the situation if they win the ball. For instance, if #2 wins the ball, can he put the ball in behind for #1's run? If #1 wins the ball, can he play a 1-2 with #2 to get himself in behind the defense?

This scheme is a bit more risky in the sense that the overload inherently imbalances the team, and there is no way to disguise the runners here. It's pretty obvious where the ball is going, and a counter will find the team trying to recover its balance on the right side in particular. The coach should talk with the right back to specifically outline that player's attacking and defending responsibilities in this situation, given that he or she is without help if the ball is lost.

Misdirection

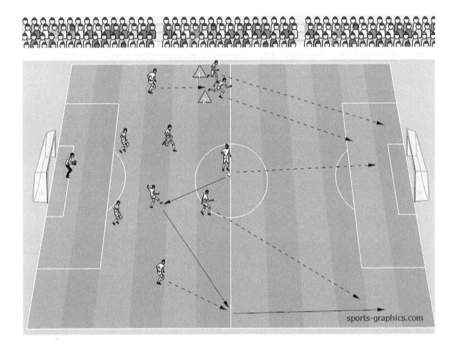

sports-graphics.com

This is the same set-up, but after the midfielder squares up to play the long ball to the runners on the opposite side, he or she instead plays wide to the near side to the outside back, who has pushed forward. The idea here is that this would be a good variant to use *after* the previous play has been run one or more times. Note that a second runner, here the attacking midfielder, makes a deep run up the touchline to run onto the ball played by the outside back, setting up an ideal crossing situation, with multiple runners approaching the box from the back side. The hope is that the defenders are off balance from the change of direction and then pay insufficient attention to the runners at the end.

Once again, the risk here is considerable, as the team is committed forward, and heavily, on both flanks. If possession is lost, the team will have to work to delay and channel the ball away from dangerous space while the committed players recover.

Central Option

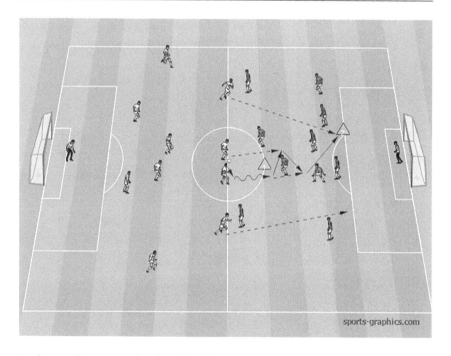

In the previous example, the defending team, though compressing their shape somewhat, is unprepared for a direct attack at their goal. The attackers execute a short pass and a 1-2 (1) and then a through-pass behind their opponent's back line (2) to create an opportunity to score off of a quick, central attack. This approach is not often successful against a prepared team, but is worth considering as an option to try to surprise the defenders. Many variations can be created and rehearsed to push numbers into a dangerous, central area and overwhelm the defense.

FOCUS ON TECHNIQUE: LONG PASSING

The ability to change the point of attack through long passing is essential to efficient attacking set-pieces. Whether it's a long ball from a holding midfielder to the far attacking corner from a kick-off or a cross served in by a forward after a throw-in, every player on the field needs to be able to pass the ball over distance with both feet. Additionally, the ability to choose and deliver the *correct* type of pass is critical.

There are three kinds of long pass:

1. Driven. The driven pass is used to move the ball to another part of the field, over distance, as quickly as possible. Height is not critical and the ball is struck with the laces along the back (similar to shooting at pace). This pass has the advantage of great speed, but is generally less accurate.

2. Lofted. This service travels over distance and most often over players as well. The lofted pass is struck with pace by using the laces and striking the ball below center, causing great lift. This pass can be used to change the point of attack anywhere on the field.

3. Chipped. This is a specialized pass used to reach a specific target, often in behind or in a crowd, and to give that target the opportunity for easier control on reception. The pass is struck with the laces, well below center-back, and by halting the follow-through at the moment of striking, the passer applies back-spin to the ball. That spin helps the pass float and also reduces and bounce.

In addition to these three types of passes, there are other important means of influencing the ball (e.g., bending) that players can learn to give them the ability to deliver an effective ball that can facilitate set-piece service.

This section contains a number of efficient, challenging environments for players to train their long-passing technique.

Driving Range Pairs Long Passing

sports-graphics.com

Players work in pairs over distance, practicing driven, lofted, and chipped passes, as well as receiving. This is a terrific means of allowing players a few minutes to train on their ability to play over distance, and a great opportunity for the coach to help the players make technical corrections to their ball striking. The coach can require a particular pass (or foot) be worked on, or allow the players time to experiment with spinning (bending) the ball or seeing who can strike the ball over the most distance. In the case of set-piece preparation, players should generally hit a dead (not moving) ball, focusing on the distance and texture of the pass required. For example, hitting balls deep off of kick-offs should involve distance, lofted passing. For younger players, placing a goal down the middle of the area can be a useful visual aid for the players to practice striking lofted and chipped balls *over* the target. Encourage the receiving partner to use the opportunity to train their receiving touch.

Horseshoes Long Passing 4s

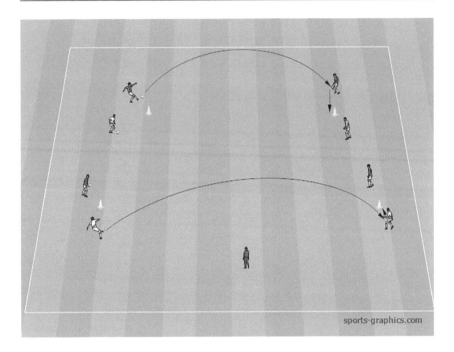

sports-graphics.com

Players work in pairs and play against another pair in a foursome. One member of each pair goes to each end of the playing area. Two cones are placed thirty yards apart (adjust according to the ability of the players to deliver the pass). Pairs alternate passing over the distance between cones. The goal is to receive the pass in the air and place it with one touch as close as possible to the cone. If the ball contacts the ground before the receiving player can touch it, the team loses that round. The team whose ball rolls to a stop closer to the cone earns a point. Players alternate roles as passer and receiver. The first team to score three points wins. To emphasize set-piece preparation, ensure that each ball is hit from a stationary position, and dictate the type of pass and the striking foot.

Coach

- Quality driven, lofted, and chipped passes. Technique is isolated in this environment, with the opportunity to observe planting foot placement, striking, follow-through, etc.

- The importance of the receiving touch, which is paramount here. A first-rate receiving touch can clean up a poor serve, whereas a poor touch is punished, just as in the real game, and a good receiving touch can be the difference in scoring or losing the ball off of a set-piece serve as well.

- Use of the non-preferred foot to pass and receive.

Defending Considerations

- As important as the tactical layout here is the mental preparation of the team. Errors leading to opponent goals off of kick-offs tend to be mental in nature. The game is either just starting or restarting after the half or a goal, and there is a tendency for teams to either ease into the game or become a bit less focused mentally with the pause and restart. Teams must learn to be switched on at the whistle, eager to win the ball back and to avoid playing around their own goal.

Typical Team Shape Defending Kick-Offs

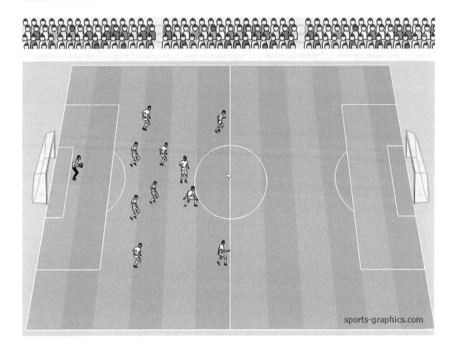

sports-graphics.com

Tactically, teams tend to compress their shape and to be ready to push forward if the ball is played backward by their opponent off on the kick-off. Compressing the team is common sense, limiting space for the opponent to play into, and raising the back line similarly tightens the team shape in front and ultimately creates an area where offsides is a concern for the attackers.

Example: Team High-Pressure Defending Kick-Offs

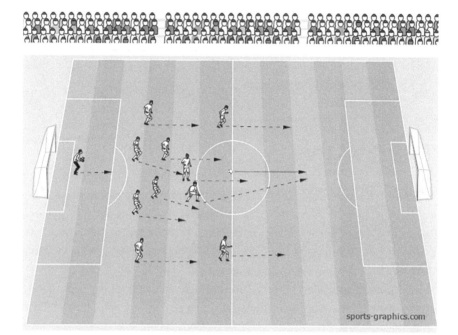

sports-graphics.com

- Does the team want to high-pressure right off of the kick-off? The advantage here is that there is a high probability of forcing an error from the opponent and the ball is contested far from the team's goal. On the other hand, a well-organized, prepared team may defeat the pressure and find that they have a favorable opportunity to attack the goal. In the example above, note that the entire team pushes forward together, maintaining a tight, defensive shape. It is also critical that the goalkeeper push forward, remaining connected to the back line and prepared to control the space behind the defenders.

- Does the team want to take a more conservative approach to pressure? In other words, some teams, aware of the attacking prowess of their opponents and not wanting to get caught out off of a kick-off might set a restraining line that is low (i.e., near midfield), keeping numbers behind the ball and allowing the opponent to knock the ball around before confronting a defensive bloc. The danger with this approach is that players can lack intensity and be caught flat-footed, particularly off of a kick-off, allowing the opponent to create a dangerous attack and set or reset the tone for the match.

- What is known of the opponent's tendencies from the kick-off? If the opponent knocks the ball around in a slow build-up, the situation may call for a more bold defensive approach. If the opponent knocks the ball long, the team may want to sit deeper, win the ball and be ready to go forward off of the turnover.

THROW-INS

Teams typically earn dozens of throw-ins in the attacking half of the field every match. However, most teams do not aggressively train to exploit throw-in situations to create goal-scoring opportunities. The fact that studies have shown that as many as seven in ten throw-ins result in turnovers serves to both underline the lack of preparation and perhaps accentuate that at first glance, there may not be a lot of attacking potential in throw-in situations. Other contributing factors may be that the team does not possess players who can execute a long throw, and in the case of professional-level teams, the consistently wide playing surfaces make even long throws less threatening. Finally, some teams may defend these situations very well, or severely limit their opponents' throw-in opportunities through discipline and dominating possession, making this a less impactful tactic.

However, there are many compelling reasons to make throw-in preparation an important consideration—on both sides of the ball—in preparing the team's tactical design. A 2016 study of the Turkish Super League noted that 53 goals were scored off of throw-ins over the course of five seasons.[v] Thirteen goals were scored in the English Premier League last season alone off of throw-ins, an increase of some 1200% over the previous season.[vi] Liverpool hired a throw-in coach in 2018. Like the overall increase in set-piece goals, throw-ins are the subject of increased scrutiny and preparation.

At the youth level, long throws or well-conceived short plays, can cause opponents, unprepared for these tactics, major issues. Narrow fields, less confident back line players and goalkeepers, and simple lack of preparation can make defending long and short throw-in plays a morale-sapping nightmare, as ball after ball is heaved into the danger zone. At the higher levels, talented attackers can often surprise even well-prepared defenses with dominant play in the air, decoy runs, and shape-wrecking extra numbers all serving to swamp defenses. On the defensive side of the ball, well-prepared teams can avoid the deleterious effects of the attackers launching balls into the area with strong organization, communication, and decisive play.

ATTACKING CONSIDERATIONS

1. Standard throw-ins where an attempt at goal is not immediately plausible.

    - What is the team's tactical plan? If keeping possession is the imperative, a conservative, negative throw-in (see below) may be the most common choice. If, however, the team wants to apply pressure and attack the goal as soon as possible, throwing the ball forward will likely be the most common choice. Either way, the team should understand the priorities.

    - Remind players that the offside rule is not in effect. Where possible, throw the ball behind the defense.

    - Where should the ball be thrown? Many players throw the ball at the head of their target, when a ball to feet would be more appropriate and easier to control. Often, a ball thrown to space will make it easier for the receiving player to lose their defender.

    - In tight space, with markers draped over the attackers, it is important that the targets learn to post-up and hold their ground, prepared to keep their bodies between the ball and the defender.

    - Movement. Whether it's a decoy run to confuse defenders or simply movement to try to get to open space, movement is a necessary component to winning throw-ins.

2. Throw-ins designed to immediately put the ball near the goal.

    •   Does the team have players who can throw the ball long? At the youth level in particular, this can be a very effective weapon.

    •   Remind players that the offside rule is not in effect. Where possible, throw the ball behind the defense.

picture alliance / dpa | Etienne Laurent

Paris St. Germain's Maxwell prepares to take a long throw in Champions' League group play in 2016.

ATTACKING PLAYS

Conservative Option

As the diagram indicates, a negative throw-in is often the conservative, safe option, as the opponent will usually move to defend against more dangerous, forward throw-ins first. This choice is most likely to allow the team to retain possession of the ball and move deliberately to manipulate the defense. It is worth noting that at the youth level, there is often a bit of risk in this strategy, as opponents may move to immediately pressure inexperienced back line players, causing turnovers that can lead to dangerous counterattacks and goals against.

Decoy to Penetrate Throw-In

sports-graphics.com

This is perhaps the most common standard throw-in tactic in the middle third of the field in particular. In the example above, the winger on the left checks toward the thrower (1), dragging the opposing defender out of position. The attacking midfielder then sprints into the space vacated along the back line (2) and the ball is thrown into space for the unmarked player to run onto (3). Many teams will not chase the checking player, in which case that player can become the target for the throw. It's worth noting that this tactic will often work well for a few repetitions and then become rather ineffective as the match proceeds, as the defenders come to expect and react to the decoy and the throw over the top. It is therefore useful to have some variants to mix in to keep the defense off-balance. See the next two diagrams for those variations.

Attacking Throw-In: Least-Marked Player

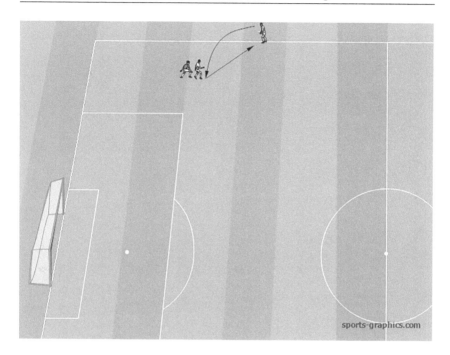

It is important to remember—and coaches like to emphasize—that the player taking the throw-in is typically unmarked. Therefore, a good tactic is to throw the ball in and then push it right back to the thrower. Note that the throw is to the feet of the player and away from the side defended by the marking player. Similarly, the quality of the return pass must be clean, typically on the ground, paced to allow the thrower to run onto the ball and join the attack.

Attacking Throw-In: Least-Marked Player to Overload and 1-2

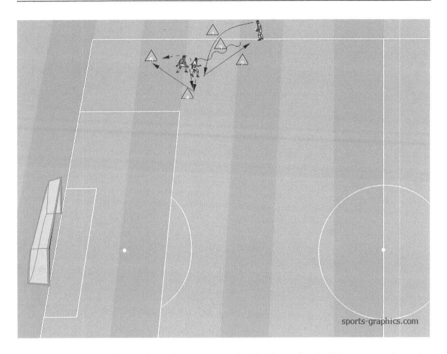

sports-graphics.com

This is a way to add to the advantage gained when the ball is returned to the thrower. After returning the ball to the thrower, the receiving player steps inside and back up-field, while the thrower dribbles hard at the defender, forcing the latter to pay attention to the run. The thrower then plays a quick 1-2 with his or her teammate, getting in behind the defender. Thus, the attackers use simple tactics to create an overload (2 vs. 1) and compromise the defense in a critical space. This type of move can be rehearsed on the training field as a warm-up technical exercise, getting the players to perform the sequence automatically in match situations. There are numerous variations that can also be introduced, from overlapping runs by the target to faking to use of the other players at any point in the sequence.

Attacking Throw-In: Variant 1

In this situation, the checking forward fakes to receive the throw-in (1), but allows the ball to slide past and into the feet of the center forward (2). Meanwhile, the checking forward spins off and runs in behind the defense, where the ball is played into space for the runner by the center forward (3). This play works well against a team that expects the checking forward to receive the ball. In other words, if the standard play is run several times, this is then a useful alternative. Additional key tactical cues are that the checking forward needs to draw his/ her defender with him/her to create space to run into, and the center forward must seal off the other central defender to create a lane in which to play the ball through.

Attacking Throw-In: Variant 2

This is a response to the center back applying very heavy pressure (or perhaps no pressure) to the checking player. In that case, the receiving player (1) lays the ball off to the thrower (2), who is typically unmarked. The thrower is faced-up and has a clear lane to put the ball in behind for the attacking midfielder's run (3).

Attacking Throw-In to Earn Another Throw-In: Part 1

sports-graphics.com

This concept, contributed by former United Soccer Coaches Director of Coaching Education Jeff Tipping, is a design for pushing the game up the touch line and into the opponent's end of the field. The target of the throw first creates a lane along the touch line for the thrower to serve the ball. Then the target, after letting the ball run, gets on the inside shoulder of the defender (if the attacker cannot be first to the ball) and applies pressure to the defender, both closing him/her off of the field and then also denying a turn up-field (see following diagram). The idea here is to get the defender to simply push the ball out over the touchline, giving the attackers another throw-in further up-field. This scheme can help the attacking team move the game into the attacking third, and can, over the course of the match, frustrate the defenders and force them to continually cede ground and possession. It's important to practice the pressure for the wing attackers so that they learn to pressure the defender toward the touchline *and* deny an up-field turn.

Attacking Throw-In to Earn Another Throw-In: Part 2

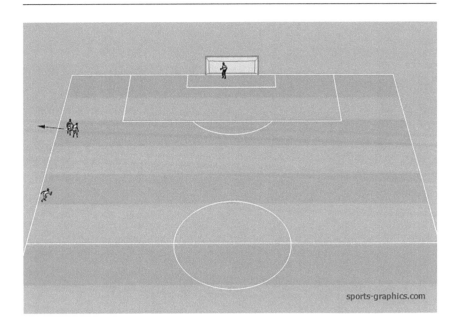

Attacking Throw-In to Gain the End Line

If the throw-in is in the front third, this sequence can be used to try to create a crossing situation. The right forward posts up on the opponent's left back, fixing this player in place (1). The center forward takes a position ball-side of the near-side center back (2). The attacking midfielder (3) makes a sudden sprint into the seam between the two front-line players, passing close enough to the right forward and his marker to deny the player marking the attacking midfielder an easy tracking angle. This is not a pick, and it won't work every time, but done right, it makes it difficult for the marker to get to the ball on time. The attacking midfielder runs toward the end line, where the ball is thrown, and then crosses for the left forward to finish.

Attacking Throw-In to Gain the End Line: Variant 1

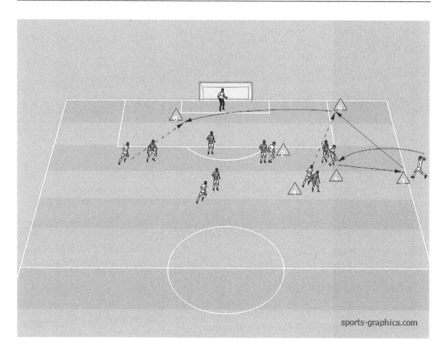

This is similar to the previous play, except that the ball is thrown in to the feet of the forward (1) and then passed back to the thrower (3) (usually unmarked), who then passes the ball toward the end line for the attacking midfielder to run onto (4) and cross (5). Note that the center forward again tries to occupy the left center back (2) to assure there is no defensive help to deny the cross.

FOCUS ON TECHNIQUE: DEFENDERS EARNING THROW-INS

Defenders Win Throw-Ins

sports-graphics.com

This is a skill many defenders, particularly those who play in wide positions, eventually develop, but it's not often coached. Defenders often find themselves tightly pressured, facing their own goal. Frequently the next decision is to pass back to the goalkeeper, but this option may not always be available, and defenders need to learn to turn toward the line and play the ball off of the attacker and out for a throw-in. Doing this often forces the chasing attacker to back off a bit, too, as they do not enjoy being struck by the ball. For the defender under pressure, the key is to get a bit of separation by slowing a bit and then taking a longer touch and pushing off of the chasing player. Then the defender has to turn and look to play off of the foot or leg (outside ½ of the foot or leg) nearest the touchline, and preferably when the chasing player has weight on that foot (so they cannot adjust and avoid) and is out of play. Again, this is an important skill for the defender so that they feel confident dealing with that pressuring player and they know how to play out of the situation. Interestingly, this is also a good training environment for the chasing attacker to learn to try not to give up the throw in. Trying to get as close as possible to the turning defender and also angling one's body and especially feet inward, away from the touchline, can win the ball and create an opening to get in behind.

ATTACKING THROW-INS TO GOAL

Check-Switch

sports-graphics.com

This play uses misdirection and a blocking movement to free up a runner to receive the throw-in and cross. First, one runner from the group checks to the ball (1), dragging a defender away from the target area. Then the runner nearest the end line moves up-field and in a direction to block or deflect the marker of the third runner (2). The target runner then sprints toward the end line, losing his marker (3). The runner then crosses for any of the three targets in front of goal to finish (4). Note the three safety players who remain in position to defend against a counterattack.

Clear-Out to Set Up Cross and Finish

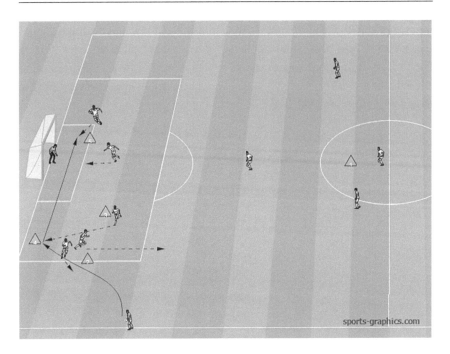

This is similar to the previous play, except that here the attackers deploy to dummy runs to clear space for the target runner. Note the use of safety players (1) near mid field to protect against a sudden counterattack by the opponent. Two decoy runs (2) break back up-field and toward the thrower as shown, with the latter running right by the ball. The target runner (3) sprints into the cleared area (4) and crosses for the runners entering the six-yard box.

Clear-Out to Set Up Cross and Finish: Variant

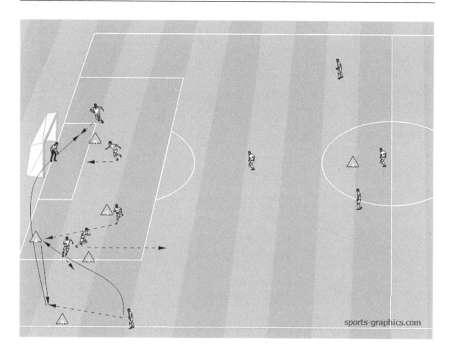

This is the same set-up as the previous exercise, except that the target runner, on arriving at the end line, lays the ball off to the thrower, who is likely unmarked, who crosses to the targets at the back post. This variant can be a follow-up to the base play (i.e., run this after running the previous play) or as a read option, where if the target runner cannot cross due to pressure from his or her mark, he or she pushes the ball out wide for the cross. Either way, this play should create an open serve into the runners at the back post.

Dummy-Set and Shoot or Serve

sports-graphics.com

This scheme utilizes a check run and dummy to create room for a set to shoot or serve. First, a decoy run drags a defender to the end line and away from the danger area (1). The throw-in is made, with the emphasis on a low, hard throw (2). The near runner, who is in line with the ball, moves toward the thrower, peeling off at the last second in an up-field direction (3). The remaining target posts-up on his/her defender, absorbing the ball and laying it off in no more than two touches. The player who executed the dummy spins off of his defender and either finishes (4) (back post) or serves to the back post runners (5). This movement takes time and the defenders must be caught off-balance. The quality of the throw, the dummy, the receiving touch(es), and the lay-off are all variables that must be refined to create consistent scoring chances from this move.

Long Throw-In and Flick

This scheme uses a long throw (1) to a target who flicks the ball (2) toward the goal. Note the player (3) assigned to the goalkeeper. This player cannot impede the goalkeeper's route to the ball, but he/she can move slowly in that direction, making the goalkeeper's path to the ball more difficult. He/she also aims to finish the flick if the ball makes its way to him/her. Two runners (4) are staggered near the penalty spot, with one crashing the near post, trying to arrive in time to smash the ball into the goal. The latter runner remains near his/her starting point, prepared to finish any ball that pops out to him/her. Finally, it is very important to place a player at the back post (5). This is the framing player, who assures that any ball coming across the face of the goal is finished or put back into the danger area in front of goal.

Perhaps the most challenging aspect of this play is getting the thrower/flicker relationship sorted out. The thrower needs regular training opportunities to achieve consistency in finding the head of the target. Similarly, the flicker needs to get used to making adjustments and feeling where to try to place the ball. This is a difficult play to defend and, once established, one that is easy to create variations from that will cause opponents further difficulties.

picture alliance / dpa | Frank Rumpenhorst

Gaetan Bussmann of Mainz flicks the ball past a trio of Darmstadt defenders in Bundesliga play.

Lay-Off to Finish: Long Throw Variant 1

This variant is similar to the original play, but after the throw and flick (1), the player posting up on the goalkeeper (2) attempts to lay the ball off to the higher runner (3) to finish. One of the challenges of the base play is that the player on the goalkeeper is facing away from goal and may have difficulty turning the ball on goal with any force behind it. Therefore, learning to push the ball back to a runner, who is crashing the goal and can apply the necessary angle and force to the finish, can be an effective way to overcome goal line defending.

End Line Serve: Long Throw Variant 2

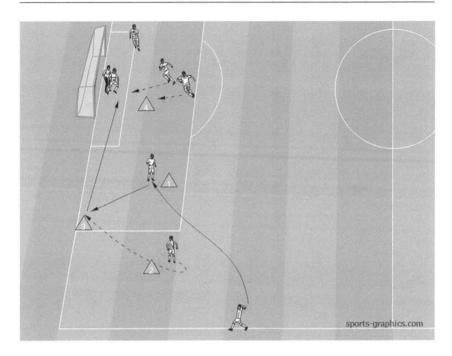

This variant comes from the same set-up as the original play. In this case, a player is added between the thrower and the flicker. This player must do their best to seem innocuous (indeed, it may be useful to put this player in the original set-up just to drag a defender out of the defending block). This time, the throw is made to the flicker's feet (1). Meanwhile, the new runner (2) makes a dummy run up-field to shake any marker and then quickly spins off and sprints to the end line. The flicker pushes the ball to the end line for the runner to serve (3) to a designated area for the runners in front of goal (4). As with any variant, this play is most likely to be effective after the base play is run several times, as the defending team will be less likely to be concerned with the runner.

Throw-In With Lay-Off and Serve

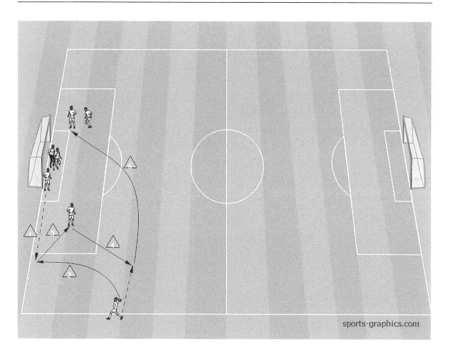

This move begins with a runner sprinting along the end line from the near post (1). The thrower tosses the ball to the end line (2), where the runner passes into the feet of the standing target (3). The target passes the ball back to the thrower (usually unmarked). The thrower takes a touch toward the goal and serves the ball toward the back, top corner of the six-yard box. Targets there attempt to finish. This is another way to turn a throw-in into a minimally contested serve to a dangerous area. In addition, a right-footed player will be able to serve the ball with in-swinging spin, bringing the cross near the goal and making it very hard to handle for defenders and the goalkeeper.

Long Throw With Decoy Runners

This is the same standard set-up, but the first action is the decoy runs (1) by the two target players. First, the near player runs to the end line and then the other target checks toward the thrower, both demanding the ball. The pattern is designed to clear the lane to goal of defenders so that the long thrower can deliver the ball directly to the near post (2), where the runners can knock it into the goal. This scheme is most likely to work well after the flickers have been used several times and the defense is focused on denying them the service.

Long Throw With Lay-Off to Thrower and Serve

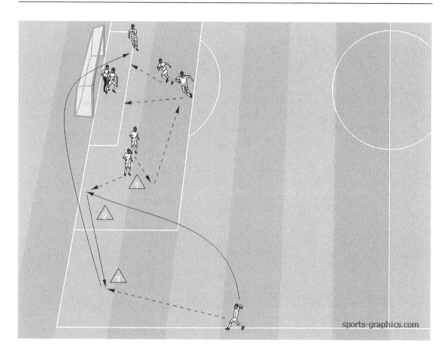

This scheme then builds off of the previous movement, with decoy runners clearing the lane. However, the thrower this time pushes the ball to the end line, into the path of the first runner (1). This player controls the ball and lays it off for the thrower (2) (usually unmarked) to serve to the back post (3), where multiple runners are arriving to finish. Note the movement of the other decoy runner, who bends back to the top of the area to help clean up any ball that is deflected away from the goal. This variant is useful against a team that has seen numerous flicks of long throws already in a match, and is unprepared for a new wrinkle in the scheme.

Long Throw-In Directly to Goal: Narrow Field

sports-graphics.com

This is a simple but effective design often used at the youth and high school level if the team possesses a very long throw and when the team plays on narrow fields. If the thrower can get the ball to the near post area, the team can send a group of four targets to that area. One runner (1) makes a decoy run along the end line to draw away one or more defenders. The ball is thrown hard and high into the near post area (2). The runners look to smash the ball into the net or at least knock it down and then pounce on the rebound. Note the player framing the back post in case the ball trickles through, and the player near the penalty spot, who looks to finish any ball pushed away from the line. It is very important that the goalkeeper not be allowed to get the first touch on the ball. This is the reason for the use of so many targets in the area, as the goalkeeper will in theory have to negotiate a lot of traffic to get to the ball.

FOCUS ON TECHNIQUE: FLICKING THE BALL

Flicking the ball is one of the least-taught techniques in soccer. Put simply, this is heading but the player uses the top of their head, rather than the hair line of their forehead, as the contact point. In addition, the player tries to either lift the ball (to produce a longer, lofted flick), or in the case of a flatter serve, some players allow the ball to skid across the top of their head, producing a flatter, faster, and more slight change of direction.

The issue here is that this is not a technique that one develops in five minutes. It takes many hours of intensive training to develop feel and consistency in flicking the ball. This is especially true in the case of flicking for set-pieces, where accuracy is so critical to the success of the play.

Accordingly, this section presents environments in which players can practice flicking the ball in preparation for set-piece training.

Static Training: Flicks in Groups of 3

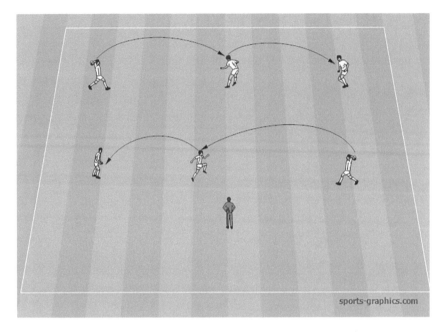

sports-graphics.com

This is a good way to isolate the technique of flicking the ball. For younger players, move the servers in closer and toss the ball underhand. As players learn the feel of flicking and get more comfortable, move the servers back and vary the serves, sometimes lofted balls that can be pushed up in the air over distance, and sometimes flatter, high-paced serves that can be deflected on to the target player.

Windows Flicking in Pairs

This setting adds movement to the technique of flicking. Servers toss the ball for the first player to flick to their partner, who in turn heads back to the server. Pairs alternate active roles and must move to a new server after each sequence. Rotate servers after one minute.

Flick and Finish

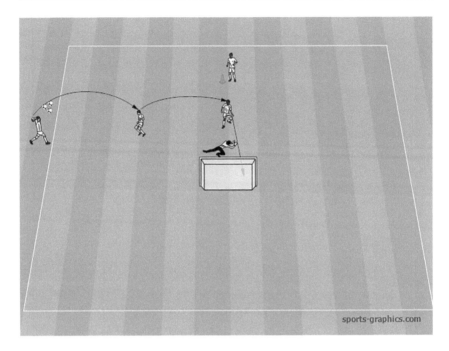

sports-graphics.com

This environment allows the players to work on the specific action of flicking to set up finishing. The server tosses the ball for the middle player to flick on to the target who tries to finish with his/her first touch. The player finishing may head or volley, depending on the height of the serve. Players rotate positions after each serve. It is incumbent on the coach to adjust the distances so that players of varying ages and abilities can experience success.

DEFENDING CONSIDERATIONS

- In general, mark players in descending order of the danger they pose in any given throw-in situation.

- Defending players try to get between the person they mark and their own goal.

- Ideally, defending players want to make the attacker uncomfortable, applying physical pressure to distract the opponent and prevent the player from thinking about their options.

- Teams typically mark opponents one-on-one at throw-ins. Most attacking tactics involve the use of movement (1) to try to confuse the defenders and create open spaces. Therefore, it is important defenders have an understanding of how to hand off attackers (see above example) who come and go from their areas of responsibility (2). In this way, the defending shape can be preserved and tight marking maintained.

- Defending throw-ins is complicated somewhat by the fact that the offside rule is not in effect. Attackers are thus free to get in behind a defending line that tries to compress space around the throw, and defenders (and the goalkeeper) must think ahead and communicate to cope with long throws that might travel into space behind their line.

- In the case of a high, long throw toward goal, it may be useful to double tall targets (above), placing a defender both in front of and behind the player. Instruct the defenders to try to head the ball back to the direction from which it came, but they must at least create enough contact to assure the target is unable to accurately flick the ball to a target.

- Mark the long thrower. If the team is very concerned about an opponent's long throw, particularly if the throw involves a flip, an interesting defensive tactic is to place a defender right near the touch line to distract the thrower. It's important that the player typically be only peripheral to the defensive design, as leaving a player open may not be worth the risk involved. However, making the thrower uncomfortable may limit his/her service distance and accuracy.

Double mark on a tall target on a long throw-in.

GOAL KICKS

Attacking and defending goal kicks are topics that often do not rate particularly highly in most teams' preparations. Yet, the attacking goal kick situations involve a useful opportunity either to organize the team through passing out of the back or immediately put the team into the attack if the ball is played long. On the defensive side of the ball, goal kicks create an opportunity to win the ball near the opponent's goal, and to channel the attacking team into favorable pressing situations for the defenders. Indeed, many dangerous opportunities arise out of goal kick situations simply because the teams start from a static position, and because a few players doing critical work can create difficulty for an opposing team that is worked into a difficult situation. This chapter explores the important attacking and defending considerations for training goal kicks as well as pattern play to win the advantage from these common, if underappreciated, set-pieces.

Russian national team goalkeeper Igor Akinfeev takes a goal kick against Mexico in the 2017 Confederations Cup.

ATTACKING CONSIDERATIONS

A standard team attacking shape for goal kicks. Note the concentration of players in the area of average distance for this goalkeeper's long service, as well as the short option highlighted by the circled areas.

- Attacking shape for the team is essential. The team must balance creating space and angles to circulate the ball with the need to transition quickly to defending if the ball is not won off of the kick.

- The goalkeeper should take goal kicks if possible. If a field player takes the goal kicks, the team loses the ability to push out right away and create an offside area, and the back line will be stretched and disorganized if the ball is not won.

- A short option. Most teams will want to have a short passing option, typically to the near-side outside back. This player must create a safe passing distance and angle to the goalkeeper. Note that the goalkeeper must always assess the safety of the short option, as a turnover in this area will leave the team in poor defensive shape and scrambling to get back into a compact shape. Another critical component of the short option is the ball the goalkeeper plays to the back. This pass should be easily settled and to the front foot, allowing the receiving player to immediately face up-field and assess his options.

- Concentrate targets in the area where the goalkeeper's serves will consistently arrive. These pockets should be well-known to the team and rallying points where players work to knock down or flick the ball and then move in support of the attack.

- Develop patterns of early attacking movements from areas where the ball will be won. These patterns should variously focus on changing fields, relieving pressure, or getting the ball forward, depending on the situation and the attacking philosophy of the team.

- For teams that struggle to win the ball and earn transition from goal kicks, an interesting tactic is to adopt a defensive posture. Specifically, some youth coaches array their teams based on the notion of marking all opponent players in the area where the ball will be served. As a result, the team is certain to have players in dueling situations when the ball arrives. Similarly, these teams also adopt a more condensed, defense-oriented team shape to take goal kicks. This is also a useful consideration for teams playing with a lead late in matches and most concerned about retaining a conservative, defensive posture.

ATTACKING PLAYS

picture alliance / Marius Becker/dpa | Marius Becker

Mexican national team goalkeeper Guillermo Ochoa practices goal kicks during the warm-up period before a match against Russia.

Sample Attacking Goal Kick Long Serve Play

In the previous example, the goalkeeper plays a long, high pass to the center forward, who has posted up on the opponent's left center back. If the ball arrives at the point of the duel high in the air, the center forward tries to flick the ball on to the right wing forward, who makes a back-shoulder run behind his mark. If the server arrives at the center forward where it cannot be flicked on, the center forward knocks the ball down and lays off for the holding midfielder, who sprints out from behind his mark. The holding midfielder then looks to put the right wing forward in behind with a through pass.

Goal Kick Long With Flick and Runners

sports-graphics.com

If the team has the ability to serve goal kicks to near the mid-field stripe and beyond, it may be useful to consider a flick and run strategy. In the diagram above, the team's front line has moved to central start positions and the goalkeeper serves a lofted ball to the center striker, who tries to flick the ball beyond the opposing back line for his teammates to run onto. An added consideration here might be to put another player (e.g., the attacking midfielder) in the same vicinity as center forward, thereby increasing the chance that the ball can be won and flicked forward. If the opponent backs off their defensive line in response, then the center forward can settle the ball or immediately lay off the ball for an oncoming midfielder, also facilitating a quick attack. The main risk factor here is if the ball is not won, the opponent may be able to create an overload on either flank in the short term due to the team's concentration in the center channel.

Attacking Goal Kick Play: Short Option to Build Possession

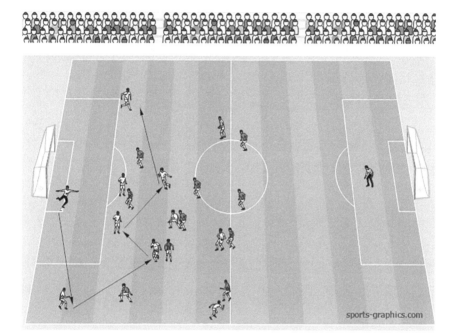

sports-graphics.com

If the ball is played short, the team typically has a numerical advantage and hopes to use the goalkeeper and back line to defeat any pressure by the opponent, often moving the point of attack as shown above. In this example, the goalkeeper plays to the right back, who passes in to the feet of the holding midfielder. This player is often the target of much pressure by the defenders, and if he cannot turn, he passes back to an open center back, who can then pick out the other holding midfielder or the left back, if he has room to play the skip pass. Regardless, patterns like this, rehearsed many times, help the team to understand how to play out of pressure.

Attacking Goal Kick Play: Short Option Leading to Direct Attack

In this example, the ball is played out to the right back and then played long to the feet of the center forward, who lays the ball off for the attacking midfielder to play through for the left wing to run onto. This pattern is an example of more direct play, but with a certain amount of structure and design, with the short pass likely bringing the opponent forward to suppress the short options, therefore opening up more space behind the midfield line and the defenders as well.

DEFENDING CONSIDERATIONS

- Most teams will mark likely recipients of opponent goal kicks. The remaining shape is influenced by concerns about protecting dangerous space (e.g., behind the back line), being attentive to the opponent's danger players, and keeping the team in a tight, defending shape.

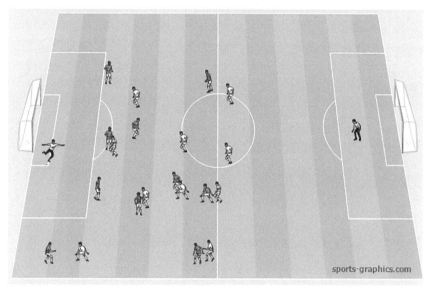

A STANDARD SHAPE FOR DEFENDING GOAL KICKS

Team Defending Shape to Encourage Short Goal Kick Option by Opponent

- One of the more interesting questions is, "What would our team like the opponent to do from a goal kick?" In other words, would the team prefer the opponent play short or serve the ball long? The shorter option leaves the opponent far from the team's goal, but almost always with a numerical advantage and space to organize. The longer option poses a more immediate threat, but also a more favorable situation for the defending team to win the ball.

- Following on the last prompt, can the team deploy in a fashion that will encourage the opponent to play a particular pass? If the team wants to high press right away after the ball is put in play, the choice may be to allow the short outlet to facilitate a coherent team response.

- If the ball is won off of the opponent's goal kick, what are the tactical priorities for the team? Many teams will want to attack the goal as quickly as possible, knowing that the opponent is likely in an attacking shape and needing time to transition to a defensive posture. Others may want to use the time while the opponent is disorganized to expand their own shape and retain possession. Whatever the priority, the team should be well-versed in both the defense of goal kicks and the priorities for the team when the ball is won.

- Opponent tendencies are also a consideration. If the opponent likes to play short, perhaps the team will deploy more players forward to take away the short option and force the team to play longer.

- If the team's initial design for defending the goal kick breaks down, what is the subsequent strategy? From a short goal kick, if the team's pressing is broken in the front third, does the team then fall back and form a block near mid-field, or does the team send another player forward to try to slow or break up the attack? While these questions do not concern the set-piece directly, they are important to consider with the team so that there is a coherent response to the outcome of the duel for the ball when play restarts.

picture alliance/dpa | Matthias Balk

Patrick Möschl from Dresden (l) and Phil Neumann from Ingolstadt in an aerial duel following a goal kick.

PUNTS

Goalkeeper punts are not typically considered central to attacking set-pieces. However, given the ability to preset a defending posture or set an attacking play, this moment is worth reconsidering. Many goalkeepers possess the ability to distribute the ball with accuracy over distance, very quickly putting their team in a strong attacking position. On the attacking side of the ball, this attribute, when available, can create the opportunity to create mismatches and overloads at the back of the opposing defense. Even shorter punts, well-placed, can move the ball to useful attacking space, allowing the team to restart its attack with less pressure.

On the defending side of the ball, failure to deploy the team to deal with punts will leave the back line, in particular, vulnerable to being overwhelmed by an aggressive, prepared opponent. Similarly, leaving open areas on the field, even in the front half, will allow an opponent to quickly start their attack without pressure.

ATTACKING CONSIDERATIONS

Similar to goal-kick situations, punts represent an opportunity for the team to get forward quickly and catch the opponent unprepared. Coaches must consider the general ability of their goalkeepers with regard to accuracy and distance, how to deploy field players to receive the ball, and what the attacking priorities are if the ball is won.

ATTACKING PLAYS

Attacking Punts: Simple Concentration to Overwhelm Center Backs

sports-graphics.com

If the team possesses a goalkeeper who can punt the ball to the level of the opponents' back line, this straightforward posture can create difficulties on the back line of the opponent. Note the narrow alignment of the three forwards. The idea is to get the ball to one of the strikers in the air and flick it in behind the defenders. If the ball arrives at the strikers' feet or the defender prevents an opportunity to flick the ball, the attacker can also lay the ball off to the attacking midfielder, who can put it in behind for one of the runners. Regardless, this scheme makes it very difficult for the defenders to control space and provide cover for one another.

Attacking Punt: Variant 1

In this case, the front line is again condensed and the receiving player lays the ball off to an attacking midfielder, who plays long into space for the overlapping back. This scheme creates a narrow opponent back line and then plays in behind, forcing the opposing backs to chase the ball and runner in open space. It's important to consider safety players, as the attacking team's shape is vulnerable to counter-attack if the ball is not won. For instance, the holding midfielder can drift onto the back line, which widens to cover for the absent outside back.

Attacking Punt: Variant 2

sports-graphics.com

In this case, the goalkeeper sees that the space in front of the left back is vacant, and punts to that area, compelling the opponents to move to deal with space and the running left forward, who drifts in before running into space behind the back line (stay on-side!).

DEFENDING CONSIDERATIONS

Arraying the team to defend punts presents both dangers and opportunities. The team must find the proper depth (based on the opposing goalkeeper's ability) and be properly organized and motivated to get the first touch and counterattack. If the team does not win the ball, players must be prepared to recover, slowing the opposition and looking for an opportunity to win back possession.

Defend Punts

This is a generic look at team shape for defending punts, with the goalkeeper (far right) connected to the back line in dealing with the space in behind. Note that the team shape is concentrated to limit central space to the attackers, and the depth is set by the holding midfielders, who are tabbed to receive, keeping the back line free to track runners and be available to release pressure and organize if the ball is won.

CORNER KICKS

Corner kicks, and the defending of corner kicks, are among the most debated aspects of soccer tactics. Pep Guardiola's dominant FC Barcelona teams often opted to forgo any effort at goal and ran short corner kicks to restart their suffocating possession game. United States national teams, men and women, developed a reputation for being highly effective at scoring from corner kicks in particular in the decade after the turn of the century by making use of their height and athleticism to overwhelm teams in front of goal. Some teams develop specific tactics (e.g., taking their attacks to their opponent's end line and, if no cross is possible, simply knocking the ball off of their opponent to set up a corner kick) designed to earn their teams more corner kicks, knowing their proficiency in finishing these opportunities will increase their chance of winning more matches. On the defensive side of the ball, debate rages over one-on-one vs. zonal marking and whether or not teams should place players on the post(s) as part of their scheme.

Whatever the coaching and tactical philosophy of a given team, failure to prepare to execute and defend against corner kicks will certainly limit a team's chance of success over the course of a season. On the other hand, a well-prepared team will enjoy scoring goals from corner kicks and frustrating their opponents as well. This section examines attacking and defending considerations and numerous corner kick plays designed to give a team a multitude of ways to score from corner kicks.

ATTACKING CONSIDERATIONS

- What types of and how many corner kick plays will the team rehearse?

- Which areas around the goal does the team want to attack? Recent research suggests that near-post options (both in close proximity to the goal and further away [e.g., 6-9 yards out]) are the services that draw the most aggressive, successful responses from defending teams. Similarly, serves into the heart of the goal area, near the goalkeeper, are difficult to convert. On the other hand, central serves near the top of the 6-yard box and back post serves hold more promise for both creating shots and goal and potential conversion.[vii]

- How will the plays be called? Most teams utilize verbal or hand signals to indicate which play they will execute.

- Does the team want to utilize a short corner option? A 2019 study noted that in the English Premier League, teams are getting more efficient at corner kick conversion, with scoring rates increasing by more than a percentage point over the previous campaign. The study attributed part of the success to increased variation through the use of short corners kick plays.[viii]

- For a short kick option, what will the team do if the opponent sends one defender? Two?

- Will the team deploy its center backs or other back line players forward?

- For advanced teams, does the team want to consider a near post flick option? Research suggests that flicked corners, because they tend to focus defenders at the point of first contact, and not the finish, have an increased chance of producing a goal.[ix]

- Similarly, how important is the consideration of a second ball? A recent study determined that goals are scored more often on corner kicks from balls won and then finished in the area (i.e., second ball) than from original serves.[x] This suggests that getting the ball knocked down in the area and then pouncing on it to finish is as important as crafty, original runs to get on the end of the serve.

- How many players will the team leave near midfield to discourage and defeat counter attacks if the ball is lost off of the kick? Standard practice is to leave one more player to defend than the opponent leaves forward (e.g., two players to defend against one forward).

- Will all plays include placing a player in front of the opposing goalkeeper (recommended) to create traffic in the goal area?

- Which players will serve the kicks?

- Is there an in-swinging or out-swinging option on either side? Research confirms that in-swinging corner kicks have a higher chance of producing a goal.[xi]

- For younger youth teams, is there the possibility of scoring directly from the arc with an in-swinging kick?

- If known, what are the abilities and tendencies of the opposing goalkeeper? If that player controls the area well, a short option or more traffic may be necessary. If, however, that player is more inclined to stay near their line, it may be possible to serve the ball very near the goal.

- Similarly, what type of defending does the opponent feature? If the opponent is committed to marking all targets one-on-one, a strategy to defeat one-on-one marking may create good opportunities. If, conversely, the opponent is more zone-oriented in their defense, then there are likely areas within that zone that can be attacked.

picture alliance / Jan Woitas/dpa-Zentralbild/dpa | Jan Woitas

Leipzig's Emil Forsberg getting ready to take a corner kick during the Champions League soccer match between FC Porto and RB Leipzig in 2017.

ATTACKING PLAYS

Attacking Corner Kick: Wave

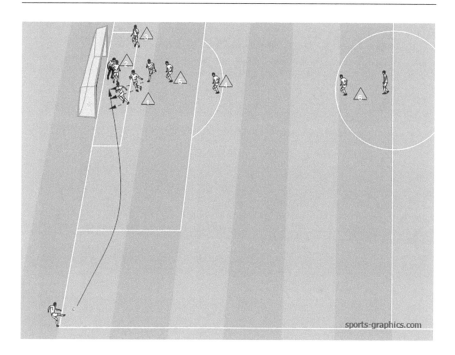

This is the most common corner kick play. Four runners are arrayed near the penalty kick spot. Three runners close on the near post in staggered fashion. One player (2) marks the goalkeeper. Another player serves as the framer, assuring the ball does not get past the back post (3). Yet another player stays near the top of the D to control and hit any ball that comes out of the area. The last runner (5) also stays in place, providing further coverage of muffed finishes or clearances. Finally, two players (6) are staggered near mid field in case the opponent looks to counter.

The timing of the runs is very important. The players need to arrive with the ball to be effective and be very aggressive, trying to swamp the defenders at the near post, and smash the ball home. The staggering of the runs allows for some variation in the timing and location.

Attacking Corner Kick: Flick

For advanced teams that can serve and set flicks in a consistent manner, this is an effective option against both zone and especially one-on-one marking. Two flickers make staggered runs across the top of the six-yard box (1). A group of 3 runners (2) lose their one-on-one markers through mixing up near the penalty spot and then they break for the far post area, arraying their runs to be able to frame and finish the flicked ball. The player taking the kick serves a shoulder-high, driven ball to the top of the six-yard box at the near post, where it is flicked on for the runners to finish. Note the safety players near the midfield stripe.

Attacking Corner Kick: Mix

This is virtually the same set-up as the previous play, with runners near the penalty spot, a framing player at the back corner of the six-yard box, a player to return balls at the top of the D and two safety players near the midfield stripe. However, rather than straight runs used in the wave concept, this scheme uses a mix, with runners intermingling, then breaking for the near post just before the kick is taken. This arrangement confounds one-on-one marking, and can be used very effectively against teams employing a predominantly one-on-one marking defense. Inevitably, somebody gets lost in the mix and there are open targets near the goal.

The critical factor here, again, is timing. If the ball is launched too early, the players will not be able to get to their finishing areas (note the staggered runs again). If, conversely, the ball is launched too late, then the players will arrive too soon and have to stop, losing their momentum and giving the defense an opportunity to sort out their marking and fight for the ball.

Attacking Corner Kick: Simple Screen Near-Post Serve

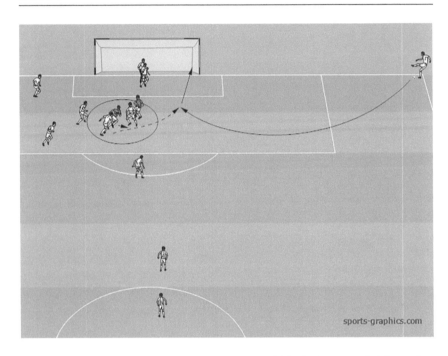

Among the most controversial tactics on corner kicks is the use of picks to free up target runners. The difficult part of any coaching discussion on this subject is that coaches generally—and genuinely—want to play within the rules, but in this case there is considerable gray area. In the diagram above, the target runner sprints past his teammate, who is not moving but whose position makes it impossible for the defender tracking the runner to maintain his/her tight marking. Referees typically call a foul if the screening player's movement is clearly for the purpose of inhibiting the pursuit of the defender, but if the screening player's movement or placement brings the defender to contact with the screening player (rather than vice-versa), the general conception is that the screening player has the right to stand or move in the area. Many coaches find the risk of a foul call worthwhile given that if a foul is not given, the target player will likely be wide open to finish.

Attacking Corner Kick: Double Screen Near Post

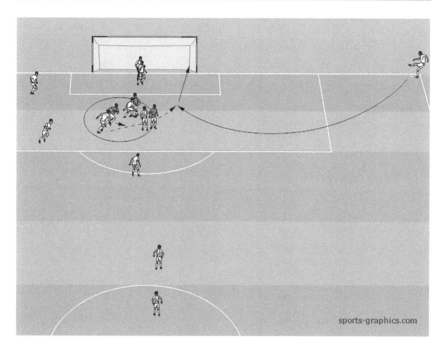

This is the same set-up as the previous play, except that this diagram shows the potential chaos for marking players caused by a double screen. The two players setting the screen set up with just enough space between them for the target runner to get through, and after that player sprints past, they can lean in the direction of tightening the space and slowing any tracking defender. Again, there is a risk of committing a foul here and players should rehearse their roles, with the coach emphasizing the subtleties involved in making tracking difficult without interfering with the defender to the point of fouling.

Attacking Corner Kick: Double Moving Screen to Near Post

sports-graphics.com

This is the third consecutive diagram to show the potential uses of picks or screening movements on corner kicks. In this case, the intention is to run two target players from the back post area to the near post area, while simultaneously running two decoys on opposite movements. The intention here is that the traffic created wrecks the individual marking assignments in one-on-one marking systems, and gets two players open to finish at the near post. Again, it's important to rehearse these movements and to emphasize to players on which side they should pass and the fact that they need to be careful about picking defenders. However, their runs can be made in such a way as to force the defenders to detour a step or two, and that should be enough to create room to finish. Timing is also critical, as the ball must arrive with the targets at the front post and be driven in so that the defenders do not have time to recover.

picture alliance/dpa | Matthias Merz

Robert Lewandowski of Bayern Munich challenges the FC Nuremburg defense, heading from a corner kick. Note the other runner and also the framing player at the back corner of the six-yard box.

Attacking Corner Kick: Jam

sports-graphics.com

This is an unusual—but very difficult to defend—idea for an attacking corner kick. The idea behind this jam play is to put runners on the goal line in the goal (1). At a signal from the player taking the kick, the front three runners all sprint out to the six-yard box line (2) and then run back toward the goal line. The ball is *driven* in to the near post for the runners to knock home (3). As always, one player remains on the goalkeeper, further limiting that player's access to the ball. Another player frames the back-side of the goal, returning or finishing any ball that leaks through. Another player stays at the penalty spot to return any ball that pops out.

This play presents some annoying challenges for the defenders. The goalkeeper rarely gets to the ball through all of that traffic. If the team marks one-on-one, the markers will be running at their own goal and on the line when the ball arrives, which makes them nearly useless. If the team uses a zone defense, the runners will be unmarked and hopefully swamp any element of the zone placed near the target area.

One potential pitfall for the attackers is near-post defenders. If the opponent places a near-post defender and also one or more players in the six-yard box near the post, they may be able to stop the ball from getting to the target area. To counter this, the attackers can move the runners to the back post area and serve a *lofted* ball into the zone, bypassing the defenders at the near post.

picture alliance / dpa | Oliver Mehlis

VfL Wolfsburg women's players illustrate the difficulty of defending the near post on corner kick plays where many players challenge for the ball. FFC Turbine Potsdam scramble to defend.

Attacking Corner Kick: Jam Variant 1

This is another way to confound a team that is able to protect the near post area against a jam corner kick. In this variant, the near-post runner (1) sprints along the end line, dragging one of the marking players away from the target area. The kicker passes into the feet of the runner, who returns the ball at an up-field angle (2). The remaining runners now sprint out to the top of the six-yard box (3) and then crash the goal as the kicker drives the ball to the near-post area for them to push home (4).

Note that if the defenders do not track the opening run along the end line, the player receiving the pass can turn and run at the goal, using the other target players to smash the ball home.

Attacking Corner Kick: Switch

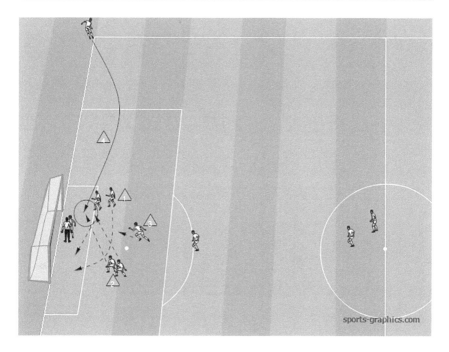

This is another play that causes difficulty for teams that want to mark one-on-one when defending corner kicks. Two pairs of runners line up seven yards off of each post. To initiate the action, the near-post runners (1) turn and run to the back post area (note that one has to become the framing player, assuring the ball does not leave the area if it is over-hit). As the runners pass by, the back post runners now sprint to the near-post area (2). An additional runner now closes to the area around the penalty spot (3). The ball is served in to the near-post area for the target runners to finish. Note the placement of a player on the goalkeeper to inhibit that player's ability to close on the ball. In addition, a player is stationed at the top of the D to contain any ball that pops out off of the serve, and two safety players remain near the midfield stripe.

The design of this play is to mix misdirection (with the runs to the back post area) with traffic, running markers out of position and hopefully picking off a defender or two, opening up the targets to finish. It is very important that the serve be accurate and timely, as the space only open for a few seconds. Finally, teams usually adjust to this scheme after one or two efforts, so it is best as a secondary option, to catch the defense off balance.

Attacking Corner Kick: Stack

sports-graphics.com

This corner kick play is ideal for disrupting one-on-one marking. Four attackers form a stack or line toward the goal from the penalty spot. Note that one-on-one marking teams will often try to mark and disrupt the set-up, resulting in some interesting jostling for position. Some attackers even put hands on the shoulders of the teammate in front of them to force the defenders to pick a side to mark from. At a signal from the player taking the kick, the members of the stack run out and toward the near or far post (predetermined runs). Almost inevitably, some defenders will get lost in the movement, freeing up the attackers to finish at the designated location (in this case, the back post). An additional player occupies the goalkeeper and players also take up positions off of the near and far posts, 6-8 yards, to pull defenders out of position and also to serve as framing players once the ball is served. Finally, two safety players remain near the midfield stripe to guard against counterattacks.

Attacking Corner Kick: Artillery

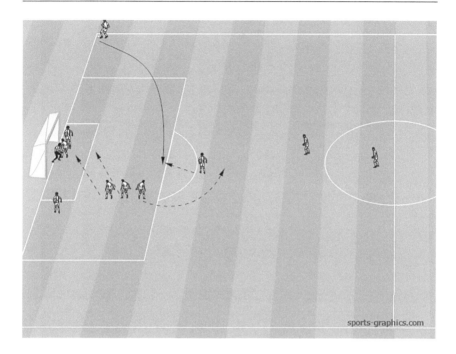

For advanced teams with a player who can volley or shoot from distance well enough to threaten the goal, this scheme is a way to set up an open look from near the top of the 18-yard box. The usual safety players are left near mid field, and a player screens the goalkeeper, with a second placed to add distraction near the near post. Another player frames the goal (this player, hopefully, also draws attention, and/or a marker away from the top of the area). Three runners are stationed 15 yards from the goal and outside of the back post. Two runners sprint to the near post to open the action, drawing more defenders down low. The third runner exits the area as subtly as possible, becoming an additional safety player. The player at the top of the D is the target. This player must break late, moving to the top of the 18-yard box to receive a driven or lofted serve from the corner. It is important in training to emphasize to the server that if any opponents remain in the area, the serve should be directed to the goal, at the near post, and not to the target, as a mistake here can lead to a dangerous counterattack. The target should learn to read whether he/she has time for a set-up touch, or if he/she has to shoot with his/her first touch. His/her shot cannot be blocked up high, as this may lead to the aforementioned counterattack.

Attacking Corner Kick: In-Swinger to Back Post

If the team has a player that can serve an in-swinging corner kick, this is a very effective means of utilizing that skill. The team uses two safety players, posted near the mid-field stripe, and another player is placed at the top of the D, charged with putting the ball back in the mix if it pops out. One player is placed in front of the goalkeeper to create focus at the near post. To add to this illusion, one runner (1) charges to the near post, demanding the ball. Another runner (2) moves to bracket the goalkeeper, standing between him/her and the back post. This is a touchy tactic, as the goalkeeper cannot legally be impeded through movement, but if the player arrives and stands still or simply moves in the direction of the ball slowly, the attacker has the right to be there and the traffic can make it very difficult for the goalkeeper to get to the ball. The player at the corner serves the ball with in-swinging spin, aiming to put the ball head-high just inside the back post for the remaining runners to finish. This is typically a lofted ball. Note the use of a framing player at the extreme right to assure that if the ball is served too deep, it can be put back into the danger area.

Attacking Corner Kick: Clear-Out to Back Post Area

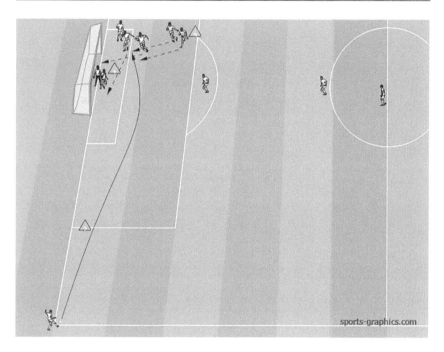

This play is similar to the last scheme in the sense that the ball is being served into the back post area. However, the emphasis here is on clear-out runs (1) by two players who leave that area to initiate the movement. The ball is served to the top of the 6-yard box and in line with the back post (2). The two target runners start near the top of the 18-yard box and a few steps further away from the site of the serve. They hold their runs as long as possible so that they arrive off of the back post at the same time as the ball. Two players are left in safety positions near the midfield stripe, and another is in the D, to knock back into the area any ball that pops out. As always, one player screens the goalkeeper and another is in a framing role near the back corner of the 6-yard box. Timing is critical for this play to work, and quality, lofted serves to the back post area make the play very difficult to defend.

Attacking Corner Kick: Clear Out and Deep Serve

The point of emphasis here is the deep serve, meant to be volleyed by a skilled player from near the top of the area. The advantage here is that it's often easier to provide this serve to an open player given that the target area is farther from goal than most, and the clear-out runs will remove defenders from the area. Similarly, zonal schemes are usually concentrated close to the goal, leaving this area unattended. However, the challenge is both to provide a quality, consistent serve and also to turn the ball on goal, and through or over the traffic, which is no easy task.

Attacking Corner Kick: Hitch and Go to Near Post

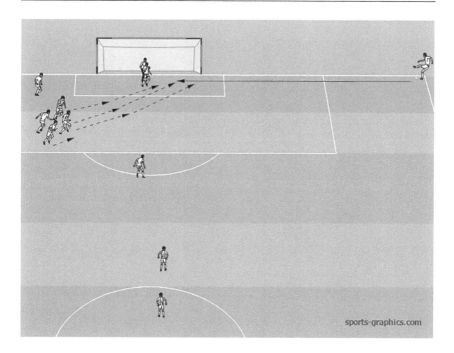

sports-graphics.com

Two safety players are stationed near mid field. A player is at the top of the D. Another is screening the goalkeeper. One player also frames the area, prepared to bury anything that makes its way through the area and to the back post. Finally, four runners are near the top of the area and in line with the back corner of the 6-yard box. One runner will stay in that area. The other three take off running toward the center of the goal area and then stop as indicated above, before restarting and arriving to finish at the near post. The runs are staggered, so as to create the best chance for finding the serve. The hitch or stop at mid-run throws off the timing and concentration of any markers, and allows the server to better time the arrival of the ball into the area. Train this play over time, so that the runner and server are in lock-step with regard to timing and location.

Attacking Corner Kick: Combine Clear-Out and Screen

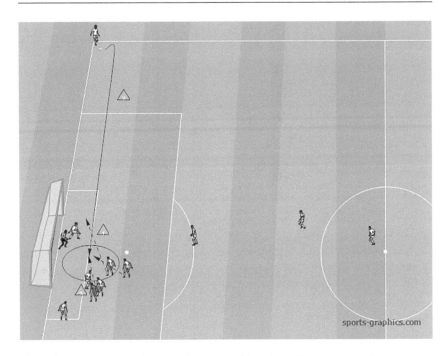

This scheme combines elements introduced in other plays to create free runners. First, one runner sprints to the near post (1). When the ball is served (2), runners move to the back half of the goal and the top of the six-yard box (3), where one player sets a screen position to free one of the runners from his or her mark. The clear-out runs and screen sets should be rehearsed regularly to help players unify their movements and timing.

Attacking Corner Kick: In-Swinger to Near Post

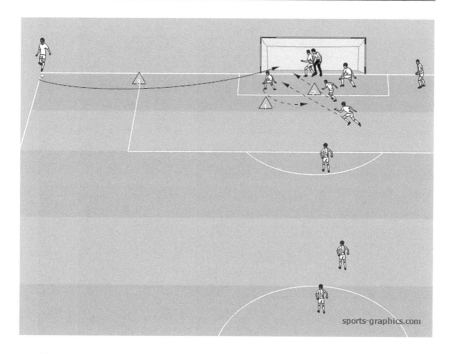

sports-graphics.com

In this case, the team opts to attack the near post area with a driven, in-swinging kick. Two players are posted in safety positions near midfield. Another is positioned at the top of the D, ready to put back any ball that pops out of the area. One player posts up on the goalkeeper and another, at the extreme right, is in a framing position to put the ball back if it is hit too deep. The action begins with the player stationed at the near post turning and running toward the back post (1), with the intention of clearing out a one-on-one marker in the area. Two targets charge into the near-post area (2), timing their arrival to coincide with the ball being slammed into this area by the server (3). In this case, the ball must be driven and timed well. The in-swinging service brings the ball closer to the goal line, thus making the finishing a matter of just getting contact and keeping the ball on frame.

Attacking Corner Kick: Out-Swinger

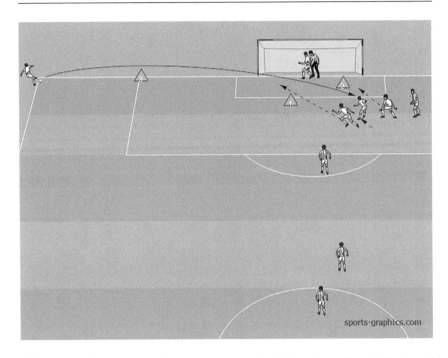

This scheme leaves two safety players near mid field and another at the top of the D, where a ball that pops out can be sent back in. Another player serves as a framer, posted at the right of the image. If the ball is over-hit, this player pushes it back into the danger area. Finally, one player is posted in front of the goalkeeper as a distraction.

First, one player makes a sharp run to the near post to draw away marker(s) (1). Two other runners (2) make short runs into the danger area 6-8 yards away from the back post. Then the ball is served (3) with out-swinging spin for those runners to finish. The major advantage with an out-swinging serve is that the goalkeeper will often be hesitant to chase a ball spinning away from the goal, knowing that it could drag him or her beyond their comfort zone and into blind, extended space. Relatedly, this is a good play to utilize against aggressive goalkeepers who dominate their area on serves.

Attacking Corner Kick: Dummy

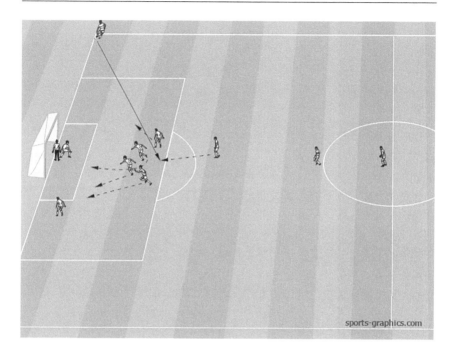

A high-risk/high reward option, corner kick plays involving a dummy run typically have the following aspects. First, the attackers put a player on the goalkeeper. This player must be careful to avoid being caught offside when the shot at goal is taken, but putting a player there distracts and occupies defenders and the goalkeeper. Two players are left back in the center circle as safety players. Another player, the eventual shooter, hangs out outside of the D, looking disinterested. A group of players start near the top of the 18-yard box and at the signal from the player at the corner, all but one player run toward the back post, dragging any defenders out of the target area. The remaining player delays, then runs over the ball played at him or her, faking to shoot at goal. Note that the player must run at the ball, further clearing the area. Finally, the player left outside the area runs onto the ball and shoots at goal. Note that the decision to play the ball toward the top of the area lies with the player at the corner. If one or more defenders remain in the area where the ball will be played, the player at the corner should change the play, as the danger of a counterattack is a concern in this set-up.

Attacking Corner Kick: Dummy Variant 1

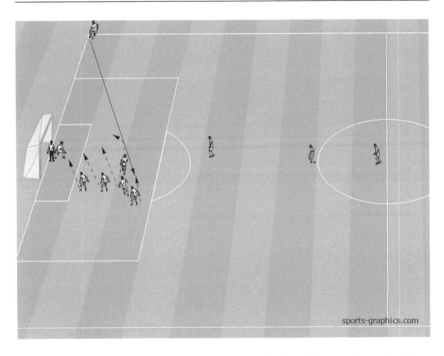

sports-graphics.com

In this scenario, the group of runners starts at a further distance from the player at the corner (i.e., not central). The rear player in the group will be the ultimate target. Those in front of that player make runs to drag defenders away and also screen (i.e., get between the path of the ball and their defender, which should be easy, given that the defender will want to be goal-side). Note that one player in the group steps up-field and runs over the ball passed by the player at the corner, before bending sharply toward goal. This set-up is a bit less risky than that in the previous play in that it leaves three players to defend in the case of a counterattack. Once again, it is the decision of the player at the ball as to whether the play will succeed based on the way the defending group is deployed. This type of play will be more successful against one-on-one marking defenses, because the runs by the attackers will drag many defenders toward the goal and open up the space for the shooter.

Attacking Corner Kick: Short Corner Kick

sports-graphics.com

This is a standard set-up for a short corner kick. One player occupies the goalkeeper. Two players remain back near midfield to guard against a quick counterattack if possession is lost. Another player is near the top of the D, poised to push any ball that pops out of the area right back in (must be shot or played in the air to minimize chances of a quick counter by the opponent). Three runners who will be targets are arrayed off of the back post as shown. Two players go to the corner arc. If the opponent sends one or no players out to contest the short corner, the players there proceed. If the opponent sends two players out to defend, change the play. In the diagram above, the player on the ball taps it to his or her teammate, who dribbles at the lone defender. The player who initiated the play overlaps the player on the ball and receives a return pass before serving the ball in the air to the back post for the runners to finish. If no defenders are deployed to contest the kick, either of the attackers can continue to dribble and even shoot for goal if that becomes the best option. It is important to rehearse the interchange at the corner in training so that youth players, in particular, become accustomed to the movements and weight and angles of the passes.

Short Corner Kick: Twist

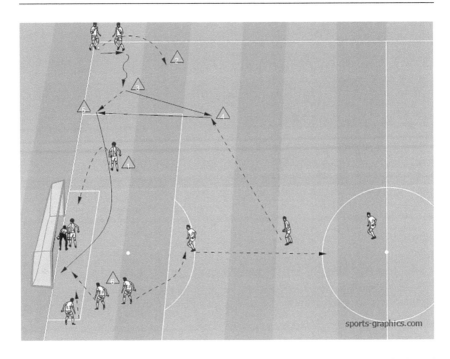

In this scenario, the team elects to run a variant of a short corner kick designed to create an overload and then a serve to the back post. One player is posted on the goalkeeper and two safety players are in positions well away from the goal. One player initiates the action by taking a prominent position, then turning to the goal line and running toward goal (1). One player at the corner passes to his partner, then overlaps him. The player on the ball dribbles at any defender posted in the area and then (3) passes to the top corner of the 18-yard box where one of the safety players is sprinting to receive (4). That player passes back to the player who initiated the play (5), who serves to the two targets at the back post. Note the moves by one target player and the player originally posted at the top of the D to balance the defensive structure of the team by moving into safety positions. This scheme creates a lot of movement and the player who initiated the play at the corner and then gets the ball back is rarely marked, so a good opportunity can be created. That player must be careful to remain on-side if the defenders clear out with the pass to the top of the area.

Attacking Corner Kick: Hidden Short Corner

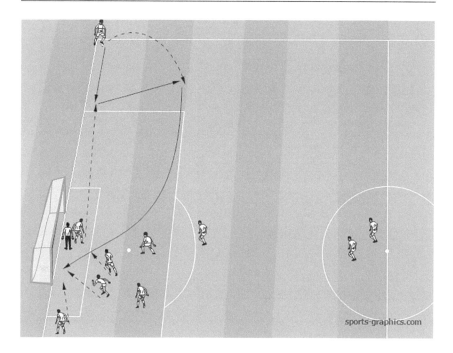

If the opponent sends two defenders to contest a short corner, or just to give a different look, the above scheme can be utilized. Send only one player to the corner arc. The player on the goalkeeper sprints out and plays a 1-2 with the server, who then lofts or drives a ball to the back post for the runners. If a defender chases the player running off of the goalkeeper, an interesting tactic is to have the player at the corner wave off his/her teammate, who then turns and walks a few steps toward the goal before turning again and executing the 1-2 with the server. This is a clever way to work in the dangerous serve regardless of the defending team's awareness.

Short Corner to Outside Back

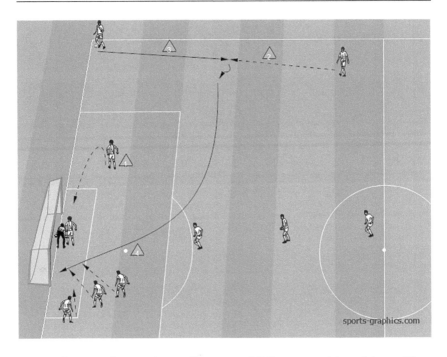

Post a player to distract the goalkeeper and 2-3 staggered in safety positions well outside the 18-yard box. Three targets are deployed 6-10 yards off of the back post. One player starts the action (1) by taking and then abandoning a prominent position 10-12 yards off of the near post. The right back tries to appear disinterested (2) then sprints to meet the pass from the player at the corner (3). The back then serves the ball to the back post (4) for the runners crashing the goal.

Attacking Corner Kick: Choice

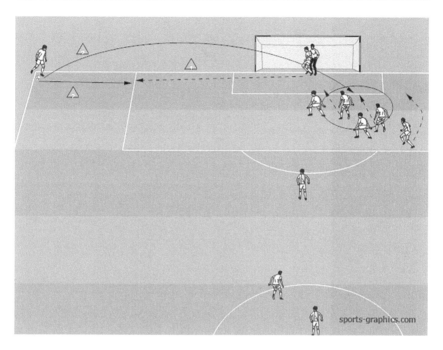

This scheme is included to make the point that depending on the age and ability of the players, it's possible to give them the freedom to choose the corner kick option that they feel will be most effective, even in the midst of the play. For instance, in the diagram above, the player on the goalkeeper checks toward the ball (1), and the player at the corner must decide whether to play to the checking teammate or serve over him/her to the runners at the back post. It might be that if the checking player is not marked, he or she can turn and run at the goal before pushing a ball to the targets at the back post. If the checking player is marked, he or she can lay the ball back to the server for that player to pass to the back post, etc. Many combinations are available, but the point of emphasis is that the coach can give the players options and then help them read the response of their opponents and choose the best variation in the moment.

Short Corner to Outside Back: Variant 1

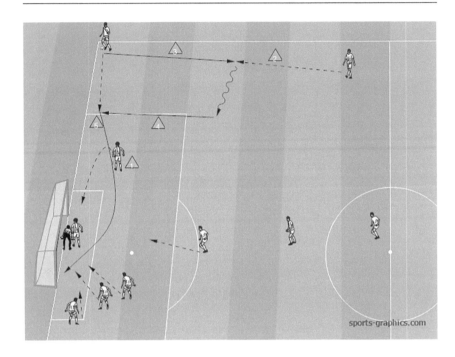

sports-graphics.com

A variant designed to get the ball closer to the goal and present the server with good options, this is the same set-up and start action as the previous scheme. After the ball is played to the outside back, that player dribbles toward the top of the box, drawing marker(s) away from the corner area. The player who initiated the play at the corner runs along the end line (be careful to stay onside if the opponent starts to clear out). The back passes down to the runner (4) who can serve to the targets at the back post, find the player crashing from the top of the D with a cutback pass, or dribble at goal if no defenders are in the area. This play is a bit complicated, but it tends to tear apart defending systems and get the ball into the danger area with options.

Attacking Corner Kick: Short With Lay-Off to Back for Serve

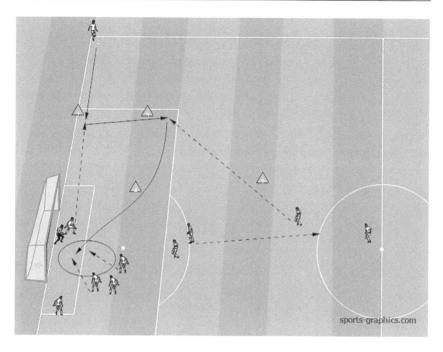

This is another effective way to draw out a defending block and create a shorter, angled serve to the back post. The player on the goalkeeper checks and receives the pass from the player at the corner. Meanwhile, one of the safety players sneaks forward to the top, near corner of the 18-yard box (2) and the checking player lays off the ball (3) for the back to serve (4) to the runners at the back post area. Note that the safety player is replaced by one of the players stationed at the top of the area, so that the team is still in good standing with regard to being plus-1 vs. opponents near mid field.

FOCUS ON TECHNIQUE: HEADING

Teams and players that are dominant in the air often win the set-piece component of the match. Whether finishing corner kicks and free kicks or defending against punts and goal kicks, heading is a skill that requires both courage and technical finesse. The following exercises are designed to maximize heading control and power. As always, the age of the players is a primary consideration in designing training to head the ball. **Be certain to follow federation and state guidelines when teaching and training heading technique.**

picture alliance/dpa | Torsten Silz

Jean-Philippe Mateta from Mainz dives to head the ball into the goal against SC Freiburg in 2019.

Technical Pairs Heading

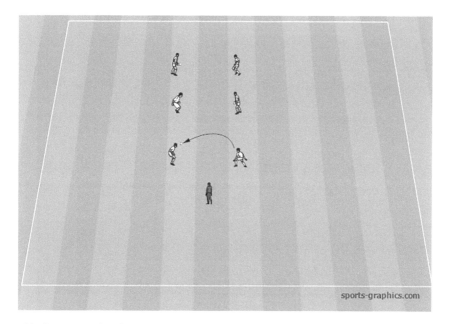

sports-graphics.com

This base exercise is useful for teaching all aspects of heading, and also for warming up before set-piece training. Players work in pairs, with one player tossing underhand for the other to head back to the server.

Points of Emphasis

- Eyes open.

- Mouth closed (don't bite your tongue).

- Stagger your feet.

- Arms out for balance.

- Shift your weight from your back to your front foot at the moment of contact.

- Point of contact is one's hair line.

- The contact point on the ball determines the direction (high or low) of the header. Getting under the ball will lift it, whereas getting over the center of the back will drive the ball down.

Variations

- Serve lofted balls that the receiving player must jump to head back.

- Dictate where the ball should be headed.

- Try pairs head juggling. Which pair can get the most consecutive (or total) headers in one minute?

- Try expanding the distance between server and working player. Can the players still return the ball or juggle?

- Try overhead service (rather than underhand serves). This is for advanced, older players only, and safety is still the primary consideration. This service is, however, more realistic for dealing with driven balls.

Threes Directional Heading

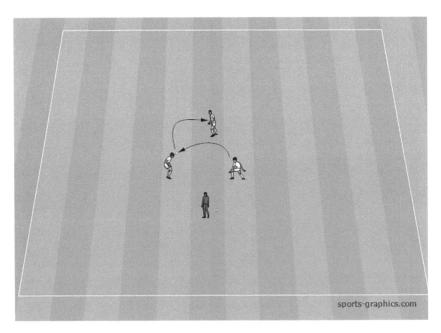

sports-graphics.com

The use of groups of three for technical heading expands the possibilities to include directional heading. Here, one player tosses underhand to a second player, who heads the ball on for the third player to catch. That player then tosses to the previous server, and the sequence continues with the players rotating roles. The most critical teaching points here are the use of a step in the direction one intends to play to help propel the ball at a new angle. Players will also learn to head the ball slightly off-center to produce the right result. Be sure to change direction and observe safety throughout.

Pairs Distance Defensive Heading

sports-graphics.com

This is a useful setting in which to train players to head defensively for distance. The players on the left serve to their partners, who attempt to head the ball back over the red cone line to be caught by the server. In this way, players learn to head the ball high and far, useful characteristics of defensive heading at corners, goal kicks, free kicks, etc. Encourage players to think in terms of utilizing their entire frame to add strength to each header, from coiling their legs to using their core to stiffen and propel their motion. Add an element of competition by seeing which pair can complete the most successful repetitions in one minute. Change roles and play again. Be sure to emphasize safety throughout.

Short Cross With Heading-Only Finishing

sports-graphics.com

This attacking training produces numerous, challenging finishing opportunities around the goal. Similar to other cross-and-finish exercises, the set-up is simple with a server playing balls into the second 6 (the area just in front of the six-yard box) for two staggered runners to finish. Given the emphasis in this section on heading, require that all goals be scored from headers. Because the serves are shorter, younger players tend to find more success here (and better, more accurate serves), and this is a great environment in which to coach the nature of attacking heading. In particular, encourage players to head powerfully, downward and back across the path of the goalkeeper where possible. For more advanced players, lengthen the serves and work on flicks from the first player along with the more difficult sliced header, which is required to tuck the ball inside the back post.

picture alliance / Peter Schatz / Pool | Peter Schatz

Bas Dost of Eintracht Frankfurt rises over Michael Cuisance of FC Bayern Munich to win a defensive header in Bundesliga play.

DEFENDING CONSIDERATIONS

- How many players will the team leave forward when defending corner kicks? Most teams leave a single player near midfield as an outlet threat. Others, confident in their defending group, post two dangerous players near midfield.

- How comfortable is the goalkeeper defending the area? If the goalkeeper is very mobile and controls the area well, the team may opt for a more aggressive defending/counter-attacking strategy.

- What is the overarching defending philosophy? One-on-one marking? Zone? The current trend is for a blend of the two modes, though a recent study concluded that mixing defending styles conceded the most goals.[xii] If the choice is to blend the two ideas, which players will be one-on-one markers and which players will sit in the zone?

Example: Zonal Defending Corner Kick

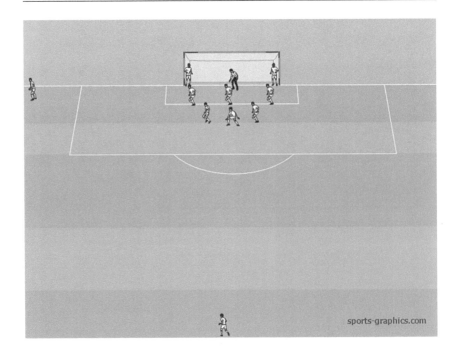

sports-graphics.com

This scheme places players at each post, and then twin zones of three players near the top of the 6-yard box and 10 yards from the goal. One player is on the end line near the corner arc to distract the kicker and deal with short plays, and one player stays at the midfield stripe to be an outlet target for counter-attacks.

- Zonal defending advantages include the maintenance of a consistent defending shape regardless of the movements of the opposition, making clearing responsibilities simple to sort out. Disadvantages of zonal defending include free runners, areas uncovered by the zonal arrangement, and static start, which often leaves players flat-footed at the critical moment.

Example: Corner Kick Defense Mixing Zonal and One-on-One Marking

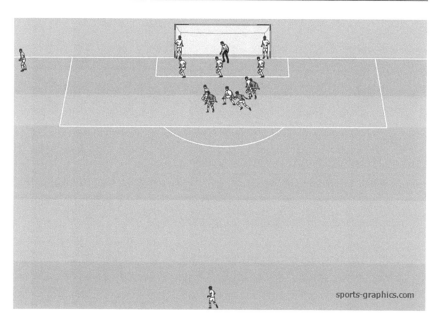

sports-graphics.com

The higher zone is replaced with three one-on-one markers who disrupt the runs of the most likely targets for the opponent.

- One-on-one marking can be effective in disrupting the runs and timing of the attackers. On the other hand, teams can use movement and picks to confuse and defeat the one-on-one marking and the defending shape can become disorganized while markers chase players around the area.

- Will the team place players at the posts? For much of the modern era, teams placed a player at both posts to cover more space along the goal line. Studies have shown that covering both posts, ironically, leads to the most goals against, whereas covering only the far or back post is the best defense.[xiii]

picture alliance / dpa | Guido Kirchner

Union Berlin score against SC Paderborn from a corner kick, with the finish coming at an open back post.

- How will the team defend short corner options? This is a remarkable and enduring issue, as many teams send no one or a single player to deal with two players at the corner. As a result, teams play 2 vs. 0 or 2 vs. 1 and are able to get good angles for crosses and shots. It is recommended that the team match the number of attackers sent to the corner and then one-on-one mark the players out there, crushing the play as soon as the ball is touched. Which player leaves the bloc to help defend at the corner is the discretion of the coach. If a one-on-one marker sprints out (above), the zone bloc down low remains intact. If one of the players leaves a zone assignment, then usually one of the players one-on-one marking will drop down in to fill in the zone.

Regardless, the team should be conditioned to look for and match two-person short corner options with a set-up that neutralizes any intended overload.

picture alliance / Marcel Kusch/dpa | Marcel Kusch

Bayern Munich women deny space around the goal and challenge for the header off of a corner kick by VfL Wolfsburg.

FREE KICKS

Coaching indirect free kicks is challenging in the sense that there are so many different attacking and defending situations. From simple restart situations 80 yards from goal to the rare, but high-potential indirect kick inside of the six-yard box, teams need to be prepared for a wide variety of attacking and defending possibilities.

ATTACKING CONSIDERATIONS

- Is this a direct or indirect kick situation? Players must be certain which opportunity is presented with each kick.

- Does the team want to attack the goal with this kick? A recent study of three seasons in the English Premier League confirmed that more goals are scored from direct shots at goal (when there is a reasonable chance of success) than working for a cross.[xiv]

- Which and how many players will the team commit to the attack in this kick situation?

- Who are the specialist players who will serve and be targets for this kick?

- How many and which play(s) does the team want to select and prepare for indirect kicks? Most teams have both short restart and service/shooting plays available.

- How elaborate should the kick plays be? More variables often mean more mistakes, particularly at the youth level.

- Regardless of the plays selected, if an attack is going to be made toward the goal off of the kick (i.e., if the restart will involve more than a simple pass to continue possession), then the players involved should get together to discuss the details. Who will take the kick? Who will run over the ball? Where will the ball be served?

- Examine the opponent's defensive preparations. Is their wall properly placed? Is there a bullet (i.e., a player who will run at the ball as soon as it is put in play)? Does their set-up leave an obvious opening?

- If there is a bullet, how will the team freeze or otherwise eliminate that player? The player can be delayed, for instance, by having a player run over the ball and then stop and point out the encroachment of the bullet player. That player's run might be neutralized by selecting a play that sends the ball away from the bullet player's run.

- How does the game situation impact the choice of play? Perhaps the team has a last resort, high-risk, high-reward play to turn to while trailing late in a match.

- What are the defending strengths of the opponent (e.g., a team with a tall, aggressive back line might compel the attackers to opt for a kick that does not serve the ball into the area).

- What is the range of the opposing goalkeeper? If this player stays near his or her goal line, there may be higher potential in a serve into the area.

- Will their wall jump? If so, how will that impact any touch and shoot play?

- How will the new rules regarding free kicks affect the team's preparations? For instance, the attackers cannot put a player within one meter of any wall with three or more players in it. It had been common practice to put a player in the midst of the wall to disrupt its placement and focus and perhaps create a lane through which a shot could be taken.

- How dangerous is the opponent on the counter? Teams that look to counter might require a more conservative approach to attacking free kick situations.

picture alliance/dpa | Federico Gambarini

Leverkusen's Leon Bailey takes a free kick against Werder Bremen.

ATTACKING PLAYS

Simple Restart

This kick has been awarded in the team's defending half. Most teams opt for a simple, quick restart. The most critical consideration here is the selection of a safe pass. The player on the ball could have played forward to the player directly in front of him, but he opted to pass to the left back instead, a wise choice given the proximity of the red defender to the white midfielder. Encourage players to be both quick and observant in restarting play.

Indirect Free Kick: Change Point of Attack

sports-graphics.com

In this case, the kick is near the midfield stripe, and the defending team is well-organized (1) behind the ball, indicating that a more direct service near the goal will have a low probability of success. However, the opponent's tightened shape means that the team's left back (2) has a lot of space available. A sharp change in the point of attack (3) will give the left back the opportunity to work with the left forward right away and perhaps create a higher-percentage chance of creating a goal-scoring chance.

It is important that the entire team recognize such opportunities, as the posture of the rest of the group will influence the preparations of the defense. For example, the right forward and right back have moved all of the way out to the touch line, dragging their respective markers further away from the intended direction of the kick. Similarly, the left forward's tucked-in position creates more space for the left back to move forward in the outside lane.

Finally, the team must possess players able to serve the long pass with accuracy. A ball played behind or over the left back will squander the opportunity, whereas a quality pass will put the target into an attacking position right away.

Free Kick to Goal: Immediate Restart

This immediate restart is similar to the simple restart, except that this opportunity arises near the goal. The white player, above, has been fouled. Although the nearest red player moves to front the ball, both the attacker at the ball and a midfielder just entering the area at the same time recognize the space left unoccupied by the defenders and a quick tap sends the ball into the path of the runner to dribble to goal and finish. It's important to note that the recent rules updates make it more difficult for defenders to tightly front the ball as they have in the past, making this play more likely to be successful. The other element that is critical here is that of surprise. It's well-documented that players have a tendency to relax momentarily at the whistle, and if two players respond quickly, this scheme should result in a great chance to score. Finally, note that it's a player running from the next line that is the target. That player's run is made to blind-side the nearest defender, and gives the runner a full head of steam, making him or her difficult to pick up for the players on the opponent's back line.

Indirect Free Kick: Backboard

sports-graphics.com

This is an indirect free kick option that uses a ball served in to the back post to stretch and confuse the defenders, and runners acting as backboards to knock the ball back across the area for target players to finish. The misdirection also serves to satisfy the indirect rule requirement. Although this is a popular indirect free kick option, it is very difficult to defend, given that the ball is not served to the goal, where the defense is focused.

The two widest runners (1) are the backboard players. They make staggered runs toward the end line. The remaining runners make runs to finishing angles in front of goal (2). One runner starts on the other side of the wall, in part to remove a defender from the opponent's goal area and also to distract the defenders' attention. This player also frames the back post after the kick, keeping the ball in the danger area. Note also that the safety players (4) keep a 2 vs. 1 situation at midfield, screening and serving any ball that pops out of the area after the kick.

The ball is served (5) toward the back corner of the six-yard box, far enough from the goal to make the goalkeeper want to stay near his/her line, and preferably arriving at head height. The backboard players meet the ball (6) and try to guide it back toward the goal for the other runners (7) to finish. Note the trajectory of the set-up ball from the backboard players, which takes the ball toward the goal but away from the goalkeeper.

Indirect Free Kick: Backboard Variant

sports-graphics.com

If the team earns numerous direct and/or indirect free kicks resulting in the use of the backboard scheme, this is a variant that can catch an opponent unprepared after they have seen backboard several times. The set-up for the kick is the same except that one of the runners is moved to a blocking position on the end of the wall (that player will have to be at least one meter from the end of the wall) to the outside of the field. The action begins with the widest runner (1) sprinting across the line of targets. Note that the other targets, particularly the most central player, stand still and get inside of their markers, sealing off the target area. The runner at the back side of the play (2) simultaneously runs toward the near end of the wall, where the blocking player assures that no player from the wall moves to interfere (3). The player taking the kick passes to the backboard runner (4), who pushes the ball behind the wall for the outside runner to sprint onto and finish (5).

Timing and a collective mentality to deceive the opponent are very important to this scheme, and this is a play that can only be used once in a match with any sense of surprise, so players have to be focused and execute their responsibilities.

Indirect Free Kick: Bypass Wall and Finish (Distance)

sports-graphics.com

This scenario is useful for kicks just beyond shooting range. Two safety players remain near mid-field. Two players are at the ball and the remainder are spread out along the defensive restraining line. Note that players step wide on both sides to move defenders not in the wall to angles where they cannot interfere with the play. One player runs over the ball to a more central angle (1). The other player steps to the ball as if to strike it but instead he/she passes to the set-up player (2, 3), who has posted up and then separated from his/her defender. The set-up player rolls the ball backward, very slowly and to a good shooting angle for the first runner to approach and finish (4). This is a complex play and much can go wrong, but it's also a great way to get a clear and closer look at goal on an otherwise limited-potential free kick.

Indirect Free Kick: Back Door

sports-graphics.com

A Lionel Messi favorite, this free kick opportunity can arise from a direct kick, shooting distance opportunity as well. Note the use of two safety players near mid field to break up opponent counterattacks. The attackers send two players to the ball and four runners are staggered off to the opposite side of the box. Note that the runners need to be very active, interchanging and distracting the marking group there. The target player slides in behind the wall and tries to look disinterested. If this player draws a mark, the play should be called off. The player on the left at the ball runs over the ball and to the middle of the field

(1), drawing attention and calling for the ball. The player behind the wall steps out and behind the wall (stay on-side!) (2) and the remaining player at the ball passes to the target who can dribble to goal (3) and finish. The group of runners also crash to the back post and are available to finish rebounds or for a tap-in.

Indirect Free Kick: Back Door Variant

sports-graphics.com

This variant of the previous play uses the same set-up. Now the runner (1) becomes the target of the lay-off pass from the target (1), who steps out (2) before setting the ball for the runner to finish (3). The advantages here are that the runner is likely unmarked, and this player will have a better angle to finish. On the other hand, there is one more pass, and the chance that a defender might sniff out the run in a crowded area and interfere with the finish. As with all of these patterns, it's very important to rehearse these patterns frequently so that players know their roles and can improvise if needed.

Indirect Free Kick: Reverse Run to Set In-Swinger

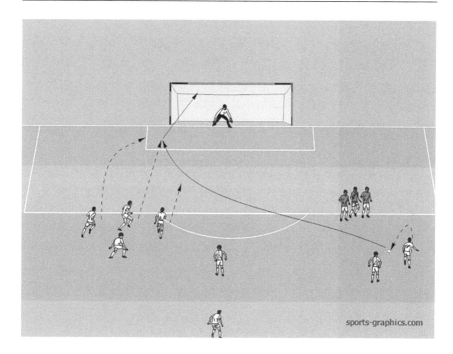

In this set-up, the player serving the ball makes a short run past the ball, intending to drag away attention from the eventual target area of the serve. The player then makes a sharp turn and steps back and hits an in-swinging serve to the back post, where runners arrive to finish.

Indirect Free Kick: Sharp Angle

Often teams receive indirect kicks from angles—and distances—that require something other than a short set-up for a shot at goal. This is a simple scheme for trying to score from such opportunities. Note the use of safety players near the midfield mark and the top of the D. The team also provides a pair of decoy runners, one to the end line beyond the near post and another toward the back right shoulder of the up-field end of the wall. Another player from the target group runs to the front side of the goalkeeper to prevent him/her from receiving the ball and look for rebounds on balls knocked down in the area. Two more targets approach the back post, looking for the lofted serve from the player at the ball. Finally, one player serves as the framing player in case the ball is served long or cleared toward the touch line. Practice the serve, decoy, and finishing runs so that players are well aware of the required roles.

Another important caveat here is to prepare for the possibility that the defending team may decide to defend this situation as they would a corner kick. This happens frequently as the start point gets closer to the end line. In that case, the defenders may place a player on one or both posts, in which case the attackers should place a player on the goalkeeper (no off-sides) and consider attacking corner kick schemes.

Indirect Free Kick: Pass to Runner and Serve

sports-graphics.com

This play features a common tactic, running a player over the ball and then passing to that runner in space. First, place runners at each end of the wall (one meter from the end of the wall) to focus the defenders. The inside runner (1) leaves to join the targets in front of goal. At the same time, the outside runner (2) runs across the front of the wall, distracting the wall and hopefully drawing a defender with him/her. The targets in front of goal move away from the ball and then, staying on-side, look to penetrate. Note the safety players near the midfield stripe, outnumbering the opposition players in the area (4). The runner at the ball sprints over the top of the ball and then is played into space by the other player at the ball (5). The dribbler then sprints to the end line (6), playing a cutback ball for the targets to finish.

Indirect Free Kick: Red Bull Salzburg

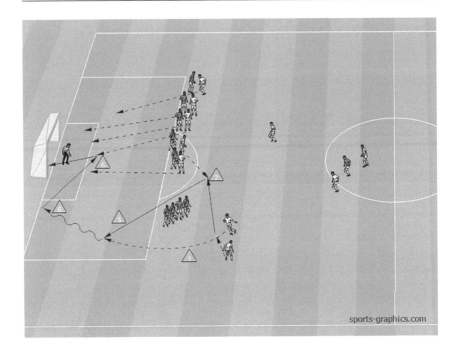

sports-graphics.com

This is a misdirection play that is fairly easy to execute and that is designed to focus the defense in the wrong spot while the team attacks the goal. One of the two runners at the ball sprints over the ball and then slows his/her jog to simulate being out of the play (1). The other player then steps to the ball and passes to the player checking at the top of the 18-yard box (2). Note that the nearest player there stays where he is to anchor and block his defender. The pass to the checking player is pushed in behind (3) for the first runner. This should be a one-touch situation to help with timing and avoid off-sides. The runner then dribbles to the end line (4) and plays a cutback cross for any of the runners to finish (5).

Indirect Free Kick: Three-Person Set

sports-graphics.com

This set-up has numerous variations, making it an effective way to wrong-foot an opponent. In the base play, three players form a triangle with each player 3-4 yards from the ball. At a signal from the shooter, one player walks to the ball, checks to make sure the wall is anchored in place, and then rolls the ball to the other player on the same level of the triangle (1). That player stops the ball with the bottom of his foot and then quickly backs away. Then the shooter runs onto and finishes the repositioned ball (2). The movement of the ball should play out the wall from the shooter's view of the goal, giving a better shooting angle. This play also satisfies the indirect rule. Note that the other attacking players have spread to wide angles, opening up the center area for the execution of the play. It is important to rehearse this play with the relevant players, assuring that the ball is placed in a comfortable position for the shooter.

Indirect Free Kick: Three-Person Set Variant 1

sports-graphics.com

This variant of the previous play uses the same set-up, with three players in a triangle near the ball and the other players stepping out to wide positions to open up the center area. In this variant, the central player walks to the ball, assures that the wall is anchored and then passes the ball to the left-side player (1), who stops the ball with the bottom of his/her foot. The player at the bottom of the triangle (2), who would appear to be the shooter, makes a sharp run at the ball. Meanwhile, the right-side player backs off quickly, opens up, and receives a pass from the player on the ball (3). This misdirection is not often seen and relies on a bit of surprise, as it takes a moment to execute the runs and passes, but if it works, the player shooting will almost certainly have a good angle and a goalkeeper and wall out of position.

Indirect Free Kick: Three-Person Set With Heel Pass to Bypass Wall

sports-graphics.com

This is similar to the other three-player sets, but with a heel pass to set the ball for a shot. The attackers use two safety players near mid field, and a group of four runners stretched off to the right side to drag defenders out of the central channel. Another runner is out wide on the other side for the same purpose. Three players are at the ball. The player on the right steps to the ball and heel-passes it behind him and slightly up-field as well for the finisher to run onto and shoot. The greatest risks here are the heel pass (be sure to have a consistent pusher of the ball on this responsibility) and the reaction of the wall, which may interfere with the shot. It is essential that the players around the ball work on making the pass and shot a very crisp, quick sequence.

Indirect Free Kick: Wide Set and Shoot

sports-graphics.com

Another three-person set variant, this scheme can be used to set the ball just wide of the defensive wall. Using the set as shown, the inside player steps to the ball and taps the ball to the outside player, who stops the ball and then backs off. The player starting the sequence runs to the ball and finishes around the outside of the wall. Note that this player's run will need to be bent up-field somewhat to give a better approach angle. The third, deep player in the triangle steps sharply toward the middle of the field at the outset of the play to distract the defense.

Indirect Free Kick: Runner Behind Wall From Central Set

In this play, the deep player in the triangle runs over the ball and then to the outside of the wall, where he/she slows down (stay on-side!). Then the player at the ball passes to the other member of the triangle, who slots the ball in behind the wall for the runner to retrieve and finish. This requires refined timing, but it can work in large part because it is very unlikely that the runner will be marked.

Indirect Free Kick: Argument and Finish

sports-graphics.com

This is a cheeky, but interesting play. The three players at the ball start to argue (practice this) about what is going on and then one of them passes to the player wide of the wall for the deep player to run onto and finish. The advantage here, if the players can put on a good show with the argument, is that the ball movement is simple and opponents are usually distracted by the argument.

Indirect Free Kick: Attacking Wall and Bypass

sports-graphics.com

This play uses an attacking wall to distract and blind the defenders and the goalkeeper while the attackers bypass the wall for a shot at goal. Note that the set-up uses two shooters, and that the kick can be run in either direction. Place two players directly in front of the ball (1). One of the players, on a signal from the shooter, pushes the ball to the side of the wall. The shooter, meanwhile, has already begun his run (2), and he sprints on to the ball and finishes. Note the placement of safety players near the midfield stripe and the wide player, used to move another defender away from the focus area. This play is dependent on excellent timing, surprise, and a well-placed first touch, which must keep the ball away from the wall and to a clear angle for shooting.

picture alliance/dpa | Timm Schamberger

FC Nuremberg take a free kick against Schalke 04 in Bundesliga play. Note the extra attackers at the point of the strike (#10) and immediately in front of the wall, all designed to anchor and misdirect the defenders.

Direct Free Kick: No Opponent Fronts the Ball

sports-graphics.com

Occasionally, particularly at the youth level, a team will neglect to front the ball in a dangerous, direct kick situation. This is a touchy situation as the rules regarding fronting the ball evolve. In general, teams will try to set their wall or a wandering player close enough to the ball to prevent an immediate shot but far enough away so that they avoid being shown a caution. Well-coached players will know in that situation that they can catch the goalkeeper adjusting the wall and leaving the goal unguarded. The rule, for the record, is that the ball can be played unless and until the referee intervenes to get all of the defending players to a satisfactory (10 yards) distance. If the goalkeeper goes to the post early and the team does not leave a player in the shooting path, the attacker should simply lob the ball into the net.

Direct Free Kick: Run-Over and Shoot

sports-graphics.com

This is the most common of direct free kicks, with a player attempting to beat the wall and the goalkeeper from a dead ball. Note the use of a runner (1), who sprints over the ball and out of the way before the ball is struck by the shooter. The runner serves several purposes. First, putting multiple players at the ball keeps the defense and the goalkeeper guessing as to the foot and angle which the ball will come from, preventing them from anticipating the shot. Second, the runner can be used to check the wall and other opponents for encroachment. In other words, as the runner approaches the ball, he/she can stop and point out bullet runs by the opponent to the official. Most teams mix up the use of the runner, sometimes having the first player to approach the ball also be the shooter. Once again, note the use of a wide runner to try to draw off a defender and safety players that outnumber opponents near the midfield stripe.

DEFENDING CONSIDERATIONS

- Is this a direct or indirect free kick situation?

- Will the team utilize a wall to defend the kick?

- Who fronts the ball? This player must be the first defender in place, standing somewhat closer than the required 10 yards (be careful!) and slowly retreating at the direction of the official. This player prevents or discourages the attackers from a quick restart. This could also be a recovering player who simply walks through the area where the kick has been rewarded. Regardless, all of the other players must use the time thus gained to get to their defending positions.

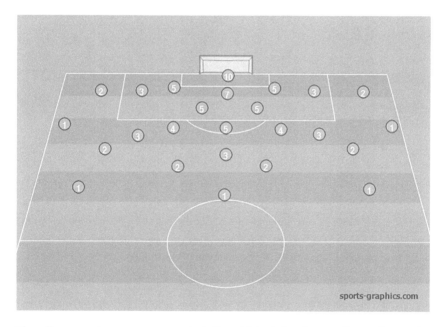

The diagram shows recommended free kick defending wall numbers. The numbers will vary based on the age and ability of the team as well as the tendencies of the opponents. In general, use more players as the kick moves closer to the goal and more central.

- How many and which players will form the wall in a given situation?

- How high, in any given situation, will the defensive line form? A higher line allows more room for the goalkeeper to clean up balls served in behind, but also more room for runners to find a ball tucked in behind.

picture alliance / dpa | Bernd Thissen

Hertha Berlin goalkeeper Rune Jarstein sets the defensive wall against FC Schalke 04 in Bundesliga play.

- Which player builds walls? Typically, this is the goalkeeper, but some teams have a field player build and adjust the wall from the other side of the ball, allowing the goalkeeper to just focus on the ball. If the goalkeeper sets the wall, that player must wait until the referee halts play to adjust the depth of the wall. If the goalkeeper fails to wait for that cue, he or she can be caught standing on a post when the ball is quickly put in play and served into the open goal.

- What cues are used to adjust the wall? A goalkeeper should give both verbal and physical cues. Most teams have the player on the outside end of the wall turn and face the goal to look at the goalkeeper. Cues should involve pointing left and right and then a hand up to let the wall know to stop. Particularly at the youth level, hollering "Left!" and "Right!" can cause confusion (especially if one player is facing the goalkeeper and the others are not...), and it may be more useful just to say "Move!" in combination with the hand signals.

Defending Indirect Free Kicks: Bullet

For indirect kicks where a shot at goal may result from a short movement of the ball (i.e., kicks requiring walls of three or more players), the team may want to employ a bullet. This player typically appears on the inside of the wall and runs straight at the ball as soon as it is touched. This player will often block shots or distract shooters.

PENALTY KICKS

Timo Horn, 1st FCK 1 saves the penalty kick by Florian Niederlechner of FC Augsburg.

Soccer pundits and coaches have debated the merits of penalty kick preparation for decades. There are those who practice individual and team kicks every week, constantly adjusting the order and encouraging creativity and consistency in their players, as well as tirelessly recording results. Other coaches, notably Germany's Joachim Low at the 2016 World Cup, lament that training penalties may at best not improve results, and at worst, ruin the confidence of the team's designated kick takers. Low preferred to look at his players' faces and interpret for himself who would be a good choice on any given day.

In Low's defense, his World Cup winners were likely stocked with capable penalty takers. Most coaches, however, worry about their players' performance in a shootout. This section includes tips and analysis for coaches to share with shooters and goalkeepers in both single-shot penalties and shootouts.

ATTACKING CONSIDERATIONS

- Which players will take penalties in the run of the match? Some players are consistent finishers regardless of circumstances, whereas others may struggle as they tire or depending on match circumstances (e.g., the team is trailing late).

- What is known of the opposing goalkeeper? A tall, intimidating goalkeeper may indicate a different type of shot than a less tall, finesse-oriented goalkeeper.

- What are the coachable variables? Players vary widely in their approach length, approach angle, pace, and placement of the shot. Ben Lyttleton's remarkable study of the penalty kick posed all kinds of instructive imperatives for coaches to share with their players. For instance,

  a. a 30-degree approach angle produces the highest conversion rate (80%),

  b. 32% shoot left, 39% shoot right, and 29% shoot to the center, and

  c. overall conversion rate is about 80%.[xv]

- Many players now use a stuttered approach to the ball to confuse and anchor the goalkeeper. Such approaches, unless practiced often, can also be disruptive to the shooter's rhythm.

- Is the team prepared to pounce on a rebound? This is an important coaching consideration in that players should understand that if they are properly arrayed along the top of the 18-yard box and the D, and they charge into the area after the kick, they may have a follow-up chance to score.

PENALTY KICK SHOOTOUTS

- Shooting first leads to winning in roughly 60% of cases.[xvi]

- Shooting order. There is considerable disagreement on the important variables in this case. Some coaches like to have their most reliable shooters in the first, fourth, and fifth spots, while others assert that if things don't go well, the fifth shooter may never get a chance to contribute.

sports-graphics.com

STANDARD PENALTY KICK

Common characteristics of successful kicks from the mark:

- Fewer errors on lower kicks.

- Fewer errors from three steps or less.

- Do not focus on or react to the goalkeeper, particularly for youth players.

- Try to pick out and be consistent in striking to a lower corner area. Many players try to hit the bottom back corner of the netting.

- A momentary pause after the whistle often adds pressure to both the goalkeeper and the shooter, but can be an advantage to the shooter if that player trains to delay slightly, making it part of their preparation.

Penalty Kick: Panenka

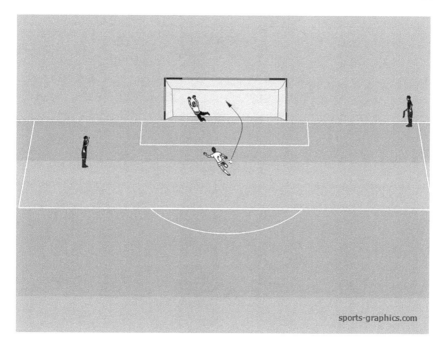

Named for its creator, Antonin Panenka, this kick is a cheeky way to catch a goalkeeper overreacting. The shooter approaches the ball as if he/she will strike the ball with considerable force, but instead chips the ball right up the middle of the goal. The off-speed, chipped ball and straight angle often catch goalkeepers off-balance and falling in to a dive. It is advisable to add a bit of emphasis to the approach, even falling away to one side to help the goalkeeper anticipate the need to dive.

Penalty: Short

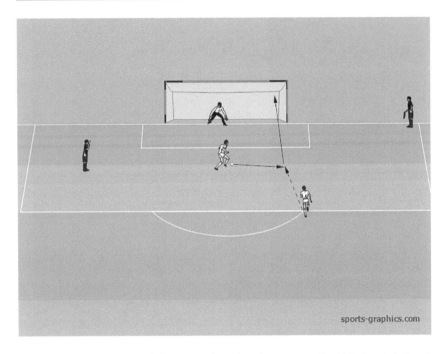

sports-graphics.com

This is a highly controversial means of scoring from a penalty kick, but it is legal. The shooter approaches the ball, but rather than striking at goal, he or she slides the ball to the side for an on-rushing teammate to tap into the goal. Surprise is the key here, as the goalkeeper and his or her teammates are often left wondering what just happened, and if the exercise was legal. FC Barcelona used this play in a match, and though it's likely to create some consternation among referees and opponents, it is a means of destroying an opponents' concentration and confidence. Rehearsal would be of prime importance.

picture alliance/dpa | Bernd Wüstneck

FC Hansa Rostock vs 1st FC Nuremberg. Nuremberg players happy about a converted penalty kick in the penalty shoot-out in the DFB Cup.

DEFENDING CONSIDERATIONS

- Where possible, do research. Professional teams use analysts to compile tendencies on penalty takers. At the youth level, this information may not be available, but observing opponent matches on tournament weekends or off-nights, or using internet video can mean the difference between winning and losing.

- Delay! Research suggests that making a striker wait as long as 4.5 seconds after they are in position (by fidgeting, remaining off of the line, asking questions of the official, etc.) can reduce the conversion rate by as much as 29%.[xvii]

- Use the angle of run-up and plant foot to try to determine the direction of the kick. It is very difficult for a right-footed shooter to plant the left foot pointing to the right side of the goal and then shoot to the left corner.

- Interestingly, a study found that goalkeepers rarely chose to remain central in their goal when the shot is taken, opting to dive or move left or right 94% of the time. Peter Cech's comment that he wanted to make sure everyone knew he tried (by moving) is instructive in this regard. Still, given that nearly 1/3 of shooters opt for the center channel, the goalkeeper would do well to remain there more often.[xviii]

- Relatedly, much speculation continues as to whether a goalkeeper should guess in penalty kick situations. The above statistic alone suggests that guessing, with a left or right dive, will not be rewarded.

PENALTY KICK SHOOTOUTS

- If the team has more than one goalkeeper, which goalkeeper is better suited to the shootout situation?

- If the goalkeeper is also a shooter for the team in the penalty kick shootout, which position is ideal? For instance, some goalkeepers will prefer to shoot first so that they can then focus on shot-stopping.

picture alliance/dpa | Tom Weller

German National Team Coach Hansi Flick instructs his players in preparation for World Cup qualification.

3 PUTTING IT ALL TOGETHER: WINNING THE SET-PIECE BATTLE

SCOUTING OPPONENTS' SET-PIECE TENDENCIES

Whenever possible, coaches should scout their opponents' set-piece tendencies, strengths, and weaknesses. Professional teams often have a specific coach assigned to training set-pieces and each has preferences and tendencies. A key component of professional-level team scouting is the observation and analysis (usually through video) of an opponent's standard set-pieces. After the information is compiled, it must be distilled by the coaching staff and decisions made as to what to share with the team as part of the team's preparation.

At the youth level, staffing and training constraints, as well as limited access to video, make scouting opponent set-pieces a challenge. That said, coaches who do extra scouting by attending opponent matches (e.g., at tournaments or on off-days) give their teams a considerable advantage, and often find critical opponent strengths that can be neutralized or weaknesses that can be exploited through preparation.

SCOUTING OPPONENT SET-PIECES: A CHECKLIST

This is a general approach to scouting an opponent's set-piece tendencies designed to highlight the detail possible and ideal in preparing the team to dominate the set-piece battle on match day. Ideally, the scouting coach draws diagrams to the right of each topic and then uses the prompts to be certain that all of the relevant information has been considered.

Kick-Off

ATTACKING

- Key players

- What is their general approach?

- Direct or Indirect?

- Any special personnel arrangements?

- Dangerous players?

- What is the opponent target zone?

- What should be our team's attacking philosophy at kick-offs?

DEFENDING

- Key players

- What is their general approach?

- Is their line high or more reserved?

- Immediate or graduated pressure?

- Specific areas that appear vulnerable?

- Do they appear ready to play at the whistle?

- What type of approach is likely to cause this team concern?

Throw-Ins

ATTACKING

- Key players

- Any long throws? If so, estimate distance.

- Do they throw toward and threaten the goal in the front third?

- Does the opponent use decoys? If so, how will the team sort out the marking?

- Does the opponent use flicks?

DEFENDING

- Key players

- Is the opponent's goalkeeper aggressive in defending the area?

- Does the team mark one-on-one to defend throw-ins, and if so, are there players to target?

- Are there areas that appear vulnerable to long throws?

- How would this team respond to increased tempo from an opponent at throw-ins?

Goal Kicks

ATTACKING

- Key players

- What is the team's general posture?

- Does the team want and try to play short outlets and build from the back, or is long service more their tendency?

- What is the goalkeeper's (or the player taking the goal kick) range in yards?

- Which player(s) is the target of the service?

- Does the team have a set pattern or tendency when receiving the goal kick?

DEFENDING

- Key players

- Does the team mark one-on-one in the anticipated service zone?

- Does the team commit extra players to defending the anticipated service zone?

- Does the team allow short goal kicks?

- Can the team build out of the back after a goal kick?

- Does the team defend well in the air?

- What is the team's defending posture after the kick is taken? High pressure?

- Is this team dangerous on the counter?

Corner Kicks

ATTACKING

- Key players

- Does the team deploy its center backs as targets for every kick?

- How many players does the team leave near midfield to avert a counterattack?

- Does the team have short options?

- Does the team disguise the short option?

- Will the team drop out of the short option if our team matches their numbers?

- What are the running patterns for the targets at the front of the goal?

- Does the team use in-swinging and/or out-swinging options?

FC Erzgebirge Aue players use a creative tactic to defeat one-on-one marking on a corner kick against Holstein Kiel in a German Bundesliga 2nd Division match.

- Does the team attempt to intermingle (or pick) to free one-on-one marked players?

- Is there a near-post flick option?

- Does the team place a player on the goalkeeper? How aggressive is that player?

- Into what area(s) is the ball played?

- Does the team have in-swinging kick options? From the left? From the right?

DEFENDING

- Key players

- How many players does the team leave up high for counter-attacking purposes?

picture alliance / Marius Becker/dpa | Marius Becker

Arsenal FC players organizing their zone-based defending for a corner kick against FC Cologne in a Europa league match.

- Is the defending arrangement one-on-one marking, zone, or a mix? Describe.

- Does the opponent leave a player at either or both posts?

- Is the goalkeeper aggressive and able to control the area? Is the goalkeeper prone to leaving rebounds or getting caught up in traffic in front of the goal?

- Will placing a player on the goalkeeper at the outset of the play disrupt that player and/or cause the team to adjust their defending scheme?

- How many players does the team send toward the corner kick area?

- Does the team send additional player(s) to deal with a short corner kick option?

- Is the team vulnerable to a quick kick option?

- What areas appear most vulnerable to a serve? Near post? Far post? Near the penalty mark?

- How long does the team wait before clearing their lines when the kick is defended? Is the team vulnerable to a second serve, and if so, where?

Indirect Free Kicks

ATTACKING

- Key players

- Which players serve these kicks? Describe the nature of the serve.

- Do the opponents use a quick restart and/or short serve?

- What runs are evident (diagram)?

- Do players running over the ball become targets?

- Does the opponent place players in the wall? If so, where in the wall are they placed and do these players move?

- Does the opponent run players over the ball before taking the kick? If so, does the first runner ever take the kick?

- Does the opponent try to use the kick to change the point of attack, or to attack the goal area right away?

DEFENDING

- Key players

- Is the team vulnerable to quick restarts?

- Does the opponent front the ball? In other words, when the call is made, does an opponent stand in front of the ball to delay the kick so that the team can get organized to defend?

- Does the team hold a high or low line for the kick?

- Does the goalkeeper place the wall, or does a field player?

- Describe the walls built. Larger or smaller?

- Does the team employ a bullet? That is, does a player run off the end of the wall when the ball is activated?

- Does the team track players running over the ball?

- How does the team react to players placed in the wall?

- Does the wall jump if a shot is taken after the first touch?
- How would the team react to a change in point of attack followed by a serve?

Direct Free Kicks

ATTACKING

- Key players
- Which players serve these kicks? Do they use their left foot? Right foot?
- Do the opponents use a quick restart and/or short serve?
- What runs are evident (diagram)?
- Do players running over the ball become targets?
- Does the opponent place players in the wall? If so, where in the wall are they placed and do these players move?
- Does the opponent run players over the ball before taking the kick? If so, does the first runner ever take the kick?
- Does the opponent try to use the kick to change the point of attack, or to attack the goal area right away?

DEFENDING

- Key players
- Is the team vulnerable to quick restarts?
- Does the opponent front the ball? In other words, when the call is made, does an opponent stand in front of the ball to delay the kick so that the team can get organized to defend?
- Does the team hold a high or low line for the kick?

- Does the goalkeeper place the wall, or does a field player?

- Describe the walls built. Larger or smaller?

- Does the team employ a bullet? That is, does a player run off the end of the wall when the ball is activated?

- Does the team track players running over the ball?

- How does the team react to players placed in the wall?

- Does the wall jump if a shot is taken?

- How would the team react to a change in point of attack followed by a serve?

Penalty Kicks

ATTACKING

- Key players

- Location of shots by kick takers.

- Shootout penalty kick shooters, order, and tendencies.

- Any obvious clues given by shooters?

- Which player(s) can perhaps be stopped or made to miss?

DEFENDING

- Goalkeeper tendencies.

- Does the goalkeeper attempt to delay the kick?

- Does the team clear the box area well after a failed kick?

TRAINING SET-PIECE DOMINATION

Acknowledgment of the need to train for set-pieces and the selection of plays and schemes on both sides of the ball are all important steps along the way, but it is the maximization of training time in every sense that ultimately arms a team to crush opponents at set-piece situations.

Coaches must create training environments that challenge players to see set-pieces as part of their team's means to winning. Training exercises must be lively, efficient, and engaging, combining the concentrated drill training of set-piece schemes with live action practice in the midst of playing environments.

A recent study of Turkish Super League results noted that the highest proportion of set-piece goals were scored in the 76th-90th minutes range.[xix] As players tire and tensions increase over the match, more mistakes happen, leading to more fouls and technical errors that concede set-pieces to an opponent. It stands to reason, then, that training for set-pieces needs to combine static concentration with match-like situations, including fatigue.

Set-Piece Machine #1: Attacking

sports-graphics.com

Purpose

To provide rapid, efficient, intense training rehearsals of attacking set-piece plays. Design your own plays and plug them into the framework.

Set-Up

Station shooters, throwers, servers, and runners as shown. Provide a ball supply at each station and be sure to train multiple players to deliver/execute each play.

The sequence of plays is as follows:

1. Direct kick

2. Indirect or distance serve

3. Long throw-in

4. Cross

5. Corner kick

Stage 1

Considerations for the direct kick:

1. Who can strike a ball efficiently (with either foot, depending on angle).

2. Multiple runners to freeze wall?

3. Change angle, distance frequently to challenge the shooters.

Considerations for the indirect or distance serve:

1. Who can serve a useful ball?

2. What is the play design? Here we attempt to serve the ball in the air to the yellow grid beyond the back post. The two wide runners have to get there and act as a backboard, knocking the ball back across the goal for the other two runners to try to finish.

sports-graphics.com

Stage 2

Considerations for the throw-in:

1. Do you have/want long throwers? If so, mix throwing the long ball into your technical training every week.

2. What is the plan? Here we try to flick the ball toward the goal off of the throw. One player is posted on the goalkeeper (no offside on a throw-in) and he can smash the ball home or knock it down for the runner crashing to the near post. Note there is a framing player at the back post as well to keep the ball in the danger area.

sports-graphics.com

Stage 3

This isn't a set-piece per se, but it keeps the players moving and focusing on organizing in the finishing area.

Considerations for the cross:

1. Use flank players to serve balls.

2. Attack the end line and serve, turning defenders to face their own goal and allowing runs to penetrate to goal.

3. Organize the box. A near-post runner finishes driven crosses there; another heads to the goalkeeper to harry his attempts to handle the ball and get rebounds; a third is the framing player, crashing the back post. Finally, a fourth target approaches the penalty spot, ready to pounce on a cut-back cross.

sports-graphics.com

Stage 4

Considerations for the corner kick:

1. Consistent service.

2. Which play(s)? Here one player marks the goalkeeper and three others go to the back post to try to finish the lofted serve.

3. Short corner kick play? Most teams have one and many teams don't defend them well.

Again, it's conceivable to add or subtract any of the stages here based on your needs. The players like this environment because it does not require a ton of running, and they get to try different roles and see if they can find new ways to contribute to the team's attacking.

sports-graphics.com

Stage 5

The final stage is a penalty kick. Mixing this in with the other elements gives it that random similarity to a penalty kick called in the run of play. The coach should select the shooter with each repetition, not announcing who will shoot until it is time for this kick in the sequence. Encourage players to try to focus on their mental preparation and being technically consistent.

Set-Piece Machine #2: Defending

This training flips the script in the sense that the team now defends critical set-piece situations. As with the attacking version of the exercise, the components are interchangeable and the coach can intercede to imprint set-up and execution at each stage.

Set-Up

sports-graphics.com

In this diagram, the set-up for a defensive version of the set-piece machine is pictured. The coach meets with the defenders to assure that roles and priorities are established. Meanwhile, opponents prepare to take direct and indirect kicks, long throw-ins, corner kicks, and penalty kicks.

Stage 1: Direct Free Kick

In the opening sequence, the defenders have built a four-person wall and arrayed players set to mark attackers and to set an offside line. Finally, one player is near the midfield stripe to threaten a counterattack. Note: Not shown here is the mandatory fronting of the ball by a defender to force the official to intercede and set the depth of the wall, thus allowing the goalkeeper to go to the post and set the angle of the wall.

Stage 2: Clearing Lines and Counterattack

As shown above, when the free kick is stopped and the ball is under the control of the goalkeeper, the defending team must move forward together beyond the break-out line set by the two red coaching sticks. The goalkeeper punts or throws the ball to the striker near mid field, and the team can practice counter-attacking tactics to the degree the coach selects. Note that this clearing of the lines should happen after every stage in the exercise.

Stage 3: Indirect Free Kick

sports-graphics.com

Bearing in mind that the coach can select whatever set-pieces he/she deems relevant for the team, this example shows the team defending an indirect free kick from distance. The team would first front the ball to give the defenders the opportunity to get their line set and mark opponents. When the ball is served, the defenders sprint back toward goal while marking their opponents and also listening for the call from the goalkeeper as to who will deal with the serve ("Keeper" or "Away"). After the ball is cleared, the team pushes out beyond the breakout sticks.

Stage 4: Long Throw-In

Here the defending team are arrayed to deal with a long throw-in. The apparent target of the throw is double-teamed, front and back, attackers are marked, and remaining players are in a zonal arrangement near the goal and on the near post. Note the single player prepared to be a target for a counterattack near the midfield stripe, and the player posted as a distraction right in front of the thrower. As in the previous sequences, once the ball is cleared, the defenders must push ahead to the breakout sticks.

Stage 5: Corner Kick

Now the group recovers to defend a corner kick. The defenders are arrayed in a zonal arrangement near the goal with a pair of one-on-one markers near the penalty spot. One player is left up high as a target for counter-attack purposes. When the ball clears the area or the goalkeeper gains control, the team must push ahead beyond the breakout sticks.

Stage 6: Penalty Kick

In the final stage, the team defend a penalty kick. The chief concern here is that the defending team organize to seize any rebound left by the goalkeeper if the initial shot is stopped. If the shot is stopped, the group races into the area to get the rebound and if the ball is cleared forward or secured by the goalkeeper, then the team pushes forward beyond the breakout sticks.

Helping Players Think About Earning Throw-Ins and Corner Kicks

sports-graphics.com

This diagram points out the simplicity of having players duel along a line with the goal of trying to either get behind their opponent or knock the ball off of that player to earn a throw-in or corner kick. This is an often overlooked element of coaching that can produce many set-pieces over the course of a match. Players should look to drag their opponent to the line and if they cannot beat that player along the line, then look to bang the ball off of that player to earn a set-piece (or a point in this setting). Teach players to focus on the moment when the player defending the line has their weight on the foot closest to the line and then to push the ball off of the line-side half of that player's foot or shin. The foot is an easier target, but also more unpredictable in bounce and easier to move for the defender, whereas the shin is harder to move or direct, but also harder to hit. It's interesting to note that this is also a useful exercise to teach defenders how to lessen the number of corner kicks conceded, by consistently defending the end line and turning their feet back up the field. Quick and short steps by the defender also makes their feet harder to hit.

Set-Piece Machine #3: Training to Earn and Finish Corner Kicks

This is an innovative way to think about earning corner kicks in training. First, a defender passes to a wing player on the attacking team in the grid near the end line. The two then duel with the attacker, trying to beat the defender or bang the ball off of the defender and out for a corner kick. If the attacker gets through, he or she crosses to the targets making runs in front of goal. Regardless of the outcome of the duel, the runners then recycle their runs around the flag near the top of the 18-yard box and close with the goal to finish the corner kick timed to arrive with their runs. This is a terrific means of giving wing players the confidence and charge to go after defenders along the end line and also think about creating corner kick opportunities if the defender cuts off the drive along the end line.

Mock Penalty Kick Shootout

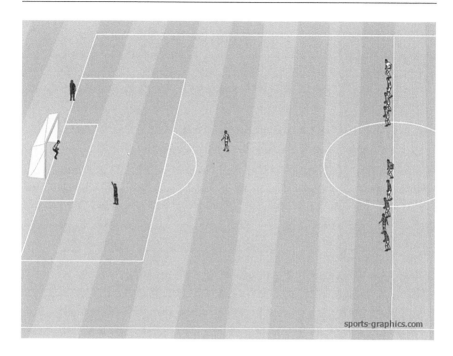

sports-graphics.com

This exercise puts the team through a simulated shootout in preparation for elimination events involving the potential to be decided by kicks from the spot. It is important here to get the details right to allow players to experience the shootout in all of its pressure-filled elements. For instance, it's important to have players make the long walk from mid field to the spot to take their kick. Talk with the group about how to control one's emotions during that walk. Many players never look at the goalkeeper, who are often trained to be a distraction through movement or talk during the lead-up to the kick. Provide mock officials with whistles to assure the goalkeeper moves legally and to govern the pace of the event. Where possible, play against another team from your club to give that added sense of competition and uncertainty, and utilize as many as ten shooters as a precaution. Statistically, it is better to shoot first, but make the team go through several rounds, sometimes shooting first and sometimes second. The more variables that can be included in the training, the better the results will be over time.

Winning Phase Two at Set-Pieces: Attacking

An often overlooked aspect of set-piece training is the *second phase*. Every team has their corner kick and free kick plays and defenses, but what happens next? If there is no goal, but the ball remains in the area, what now? What if the ball pops out to mid field, but possession is immediately regained? Very few teams train for this moment, but think about the conditions and the possibilities. First, the opponent's shape, in all likelihood, is still contorted into whatever configuration they felt best for defending the set-piece, so they are likely not in their standard shape, and the possibility that they are not prepared to defend an organized, second effort is very real. The message, then, is that often there will be a second chance when a set-piece in the front half in particular does not produce a goal, and that as coaches we must prepare our teams to have a secondary approach to any set-piece that returns the ball to our team in a favorable attacking position.

Winning Phase 2: Corner Kick Attacking

In this scenario, the team trains attacking corner kick plays. In the diagram above, the goalkeeper handles the serve, and then the coach plays in a ball to anywhere in the front third, simulating the creation of a second chance situation. The team must get to the ball and score as quickly as possible.

Coaching Points of Emphasis

- Must have the next touch on the ball in any second chance situation.

- The ball must be put back in to the area, preferably through or behind a forward-rushing opponent group, as soon as possible.

- All runs in the area must be recycled. In other words, players must move to stay on-side and also get free to finish another service.

- Any negative ball must be from a no-choice situation, and must be followed by a positive serve, preferably in the air so that it is unlikely to result in a deflection and immediate counterattack.

- If the second ball can be played out to the wide player who served the corner kick, that player will likely be open and in a good position to serve.

- When the sequence ends, players must recover beyond the cone line.

Winning Phase 2: Corner Kick Attacking Variation

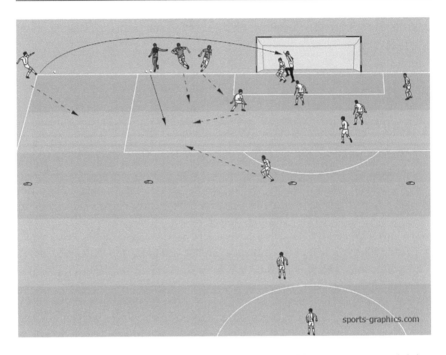

sports-graphics.com

This is a possible progression of the previous slide, with two opponents joining the exercise for the second phase. Again, the coach can vary the time and location of the second service, and the number and location of the opponents entering the fray.

Winning Phase 2: Punts and Goal Kicks

sports-graphics.com

Among the most difficult set-pieces to win outright is the service from a punt or goal kick. Attacking targets play with their backs to defenders and it's very difficult to play a positive first touch unless the ball is flicked. However, because defenders often get the first touch in this situation, there are many opportunities to look to win the second phase. In the diagram above, the goalkeeper punts or takes goal kicks to his/her condensed front three, who try to flick the ball in behind the defenders' line. If they are successful, the coach plays a ball into the grid and the attackers try to find a pass in behind the defenders' back line on the grid. No attackers can go beyond the grid end line until the ball is played there. The defenders try to win the original ball and pass into the counter goal stationed between the 18-yard box and the center circle. This exercise simulates a crucial set-piece moment that occurs frequently in every match, and players from both teams learn from playing in this environment that the goal kick or punt may be won, or they may have to work to win possession if they are unsuccessful at the outset.

Winning Phase Two at Set-Pieces: Defending

If there are considerable advantages to training one's team to win the second phase of attacking set-pieces, there are similar potential rewards to thinking about and controlling second phases of defending set-pieces. For instance, if a team is able to clear a serve from their 18-yard box from a corner kick, but then fails to follow-up and win the next ball, it is very likely that the attackers will throw another dangerous ball into the area again. Secondly, most attacking teams will have sent numbers forward into the area—including some of their tall, back line players in many cases—to try to create mismatches near the goal. Therefore, if the team defends a set-piece and then wins the second ball, there may be a transition opportunity to go forward and counterattack if the team is properly prepared.

picture alliance / dpa | Frank Rumpenhorst

Frankfurt's goalkeeper Desiree Schumann makes a save in front of her before Wolfsburg's Babette Peter (R) is able to perform a header. The sequence clearly left Frankfurt with more work to do in defending in front of their goal.

Second-Chance Defending: Free Kicks

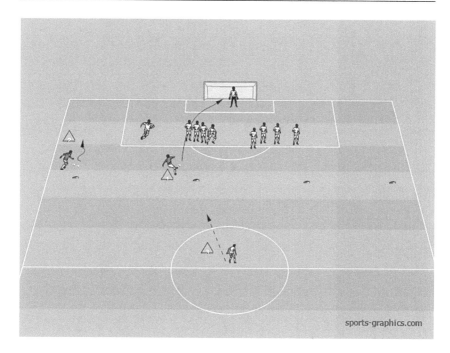

sports-graphics.com

Here the team defends a free kick and when the save is made, a second chance sequence is initiated by an opponent who dribbles up the flank (2) and serves into the area. The team must work to pressure the server of the second ball and also drop into the area in front of the goal to defend the cross. Then, the players work get the ball to the target player checking from the center circle area. Finally, the field players must all push out of the area and beyond the cone line to end the sequence. In this way, the team learns to defend beyond the initial chance and also to work together with a plan in transition.

Second-Chance Defending: Goal Kicks

Play 5 vs. 5 plus the goalkeeper. The goalkeeper takes goal kicks to initiate each sequence. The goalkeeper's teammates try to win the ball and score in the counter goals at the midfield stripe. The target team tries to win the ball off of the goal kick and get the ball back to the goalkeeper to score a point. If the defending team does not win the ball, they redouble their efforts to avoid allowing a shot at the counter goals and to take the ball off of the attackers. If the ball is knocked out of play at any time, the coach can randomly insert a ball to simulate a second-chance opportunity. This sequence helps players understand that defending goal kicks is not a one-chance situation, but rather a concerted effort to deny the opponent possession, regardless of the outcome of the initial serve.

4 CONCLUSION

There is nearly universal agreement among coaches that set-pieces, both attacking and defending, are absolutely central to the success of any soccer team. However, teaching resources for this important facet of the game are very limited, and coaches tend not to prioritize set-piece coaching for this reason and because set-piece training can be a static, dry training topic. The purpose of this book has been to examine the immense potential of set-piece training to impact the team's performance and also the means to make the training more engaging and effective for coaches and players.

Good wishes for your coaching.

–Tony Englund

SOURCES AND RECOMMENDED READING

INTERVIEWS

John Pascarella, Head Coach, Oklahoma City Energy (USL)

Jeff Tipping, United Soccer Coaches Director of Coaching Education Emeritus

Nathan Klonecki, Executive Director, St. Croix Soccer Club

Russell Schouweiler, Head Women's Soccer Coach, Luther College

PRINT AND FIELD SESSIONS

Ancelotti, Carlo. *Quiet Leadership: Winning Hearts, Minds, and Matches.* Penguin, 2016.

_____. *The Beautiful Games of an Ordinary Genius.* Rizzoli, 2010.

Anderson, Chris and David Sally. *The Numbers Game: Why Everything You Know About Soccer is Wrong.* Penguin, 2013.

Athanasios, Terzis. *Jurgen Klopp's Defending Tactics.* Soccer Tutor, 2015.

_____. Marcelo Bielsa: *Coaching Build Up Play Against High Pressing Teams.* Soccer Tutor, 2017.

Balague, Guillem. *Pep Guardiola: Another Way of Winning. The Biography.* Orion, 2012.

Bangsbo, Jens and Birger Peitersen. *Fitness Training in Soccer – A Scientific Approach.* Reedswain, 2003.

_____. *Defensive Soccer Tactics.* Human Kinetics, 2002.

Barney, Andy. *Training Soccer Legends.* Soccer Excellence, 2006.

Bate, Dick and Ian Jeffreys. *Soccer Speed.* Human Kinetics, 2015.

_____. *Coaching Advanced Soccer Players: 40 Training Games and Exercises.* Reedswain, 1999.

Beale, Michael. *The Socccer Academy: 100 Defending Practices and Small Sided Games.* Reedswain, 2007.

_____. *The Soccer Academy: 140 Overload Games and Finishing Practices.* Reedswain, 2007.

_____. *Training Creative Goalscorers.* World Class Coaching, 2008.

Beswick, Bill. *One Goal: The Mindset of Winning Soccer Teams.* Human Kinetics, 2016.

Bisanz, Gero, and Norbert Vieth. *Success in Soccer Volume 2: Advanced Training.* Phillipka-Sportverlag, 2002.

Blank, Dan. *High Pressure: How to Win Soccer Games by Smothering Your Opponent.* Dan Blank, 2017.

_____. *Shutout Pizza: Smarter Soccer Defending for Players and Coaches.* Soccer IQ, 2014.

_____. *Soccer IQ: Volume I.* Dan Blank, 2012.

_____. *Soccer IQ: Volume 2.* Dan Blank, 2013.

Borbely, Laco, Peter Ganczner, Andi Singer and Jaroslav Hrebik. *All About Pressing in Soccer.* Meyer & Meyer, 2018.

Calvin, Michael. *Living on the Volcano The Secrets of Surviving as a Football Manager.* Century, 2015.

_____. *No Hunger in Paradise.* Century, 2017.

Carson, Mike. *The Manager: Inside the Minds of Football's Leaders.* Bloomsbury, 2013.

Cox, Michael. The Mixer: The Story of Premier League Tactics from Route One to False Nines. Harper Collins, 2017.

_____. *Zonal Marking: From Ajax to Zidane, the Making of Modern Soccer.* Bold Type Books, 2019.

Crothers, Tim. *The Man Watching: A Biography of Anson Dorrance.* Sports Media Group, 2006.

Cruyff, Johan. *My Turn: A Life of Total Football.* Nation Books, 2016.

Dicicco, Tony and Hacker, Colleen. *Catch Them Being Good.* Penguin, 2002.

Dorrance, Anson. *Training Soccer Champions.* JTC Sports, 1996.

Dost, Harry, Hans-Dieter te Poel and Peter Hyballa. *Soccer Functional Fitness Training.* Meyer & Meyer, 2016.

Dure, Beau. *Long-Range Goals: The Success Story of Major League Soccer.* Potomac Books, 2010.

Englund, Tony. *Goalie Wars! Goalkeeper Training in a Competitive Environment.* World Class Coaching, 2010.

_____. *Players' Roles and Responsibilities in the 4-3-3: Attacking.* World Class Coaching, 2011.

_____. *Players' Roles and Responsibilities in the 4-3-3: Defending.* World Class Coaching, 2011.

_____. *Style and Domination: A Tactical Analysis of FC Barcelona.* World Class Coaching, 2012.

_____. *The Art of the Duel: Elite 1 vs. 1 Training.* Foreword by Anson Dorrance. World Class Coaching, 2014.

_____. *Competitive Small Group Training: Maximizing Player Development in the Small GrouSetting.* Foreword by Tony Sanneh. World Class Coaching, 2014.

_____. Complete Soccer Coaching Curriculum for 3-18 Year Old Players Volume I. NSCAA, 2014 (contributor).

_____, John Pascarella. *Soccer Goalkeeper Training: The Comprehensive Guide.* Meyer & Meyer, 2017.

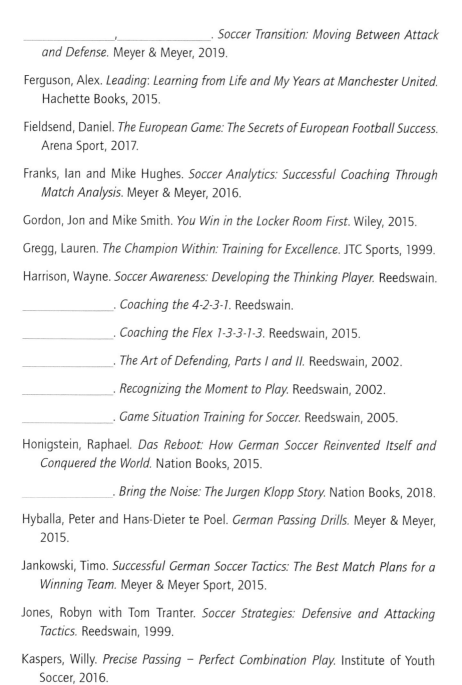

_____,_____. *Soccer Transition: Moving Between Attack and Defense*. Meyer & Meyer, 2019.

Ferguson, Alex. *Leading: Learning from Life and My Years at Manchester United*. Hachette Books, 2015.

Fieldsend, Daniel. *The European Game: The Secrets of European Football Success*. Arena Sport, 2017.

Franks, Ian and Mike Hughes. *Soccer Analytics: Successful Coaching Through Match Analysis*. Meyer & Meyer, 2016.

Gordon, Jon and Mike Smith. *You Win in the Locker Room First*. Wiley, 2015.

Gregg, Lauren. *The Champion Within: Training for Excellence*. JTC Sports, 1999.

Harrison, Wayne. *Soccer Awareness: Developing the Thinking Player*. Reedswain.

_____. *Coaching the 4-2-3-1*. Reedswain.

_____. *Coaching the Flex 1-3-3-1-3*. Reedswain, 2015.

_____. *The Art of Defending, Parts I and II*. Reedswain, 2002.

_____. *Recognizing the Moment to Play*. Reedswain, 2002.

_____. *Game Situation Training for Soccer*. Reedswain, 2005.

Honigstein, Raphael. *Das Reboot: How German Soccer Reinvented Itself and Conquered the World*. Nation Books, 2015.

_____. *Bring the Noise: The Jurgen Klopp Story*. Nation Books, 2018.

Hyballa, Peter and Hans-Dieter te Poel. *German Passing Drills*. Meyer & Meyer, 2015.

Jankowski, Timo. *Successful German Soccer Tactics: The Best Match Plans for a Winning Team*. Meyer & Meyer Sport, 2015.

Jones, Robyn with Tom Tranter. *Soccer Strategies: Defensive and Attacking Tactics*. Reedswain, 1999.

Kaspers, Willy. *Precise Passing – Perfect Combination Play*. Institute of Youth Soccer, 2016.

Kouns, Chris. *Counter Attacking in the Modern Game*. World Class Coaching, 2016.

Lloyd, Carli. *When Nobody was Watching: My Hard-Fought Journey to the Top of the Soccer World*. Houghton Mifflin Harcourt, 2016.

Lucchesi, Massimo. *Pressing*. Reedswain, 2003.

Luxbacher, Joseph A. *Attacking Soccer: Tactics and Drills for High-Scoring Offense*. Human Kinetics, 1999.

Lyttleton, Ben. *Twelve Yards: The Art and Psychology of the Perfect Penalty Kick*. Penguin, 2014.

Neveling, Elmar. *Jurgen Klopp: The Biography*. Ebury Press, 2016.

Perarnau, Marti. *Pep Confidential: The Inside Story of Pep Guardiola's First Season at Bayern Munich*. Arena, 2014.

_____. *Pep Guardiola: The Evolution*. Arena, 2016.

Pascarella, John. Field session, 2016 NSCAA Convention.

_____. Field and Classroom presentations, NSCAA Master Coach Certificate, 2015.

Power, Paul, Jennifer Hobbs, Hector Ruiz, Xinyu Wei and Patrick Lucey. *Mythbusting Set-Pieces in Soccer*. 2018 Research Papers Competition Presented by Major League Baseball.

Pulling, Craig. 'Long Corner Kicks in the English Premier League: Deliveries into the Goal Area and Critical Area.' *Kinesiology* 47 (2015).

Rivoire, Xavier. *Arsene Wenger: The Biography*. Aurum, 2007.

Roscoe, Phil and Mike Vincent. *Modern Attacking & Goal Scoring*. World Class Coaching, 2010.

Schreiner, Peter. *Tactical Games – Part I*. Institute of Youth Soccer, 2018.

_____. *Tactical Games – Part 2*. Institute of Youth Soccer, 2018.

Seeger, Fabian. *Creative Soccer Training*. Mayer & Mayer, 2017.

Tipping, Jeff. *Drills and Exercises to Develop the Elite American Player*. Jeff Tipping, 2012.

_____. Session presentations at the NSCAA Conventions.

Toplardan, Duran. *Quantitative Analysis of Goals Scored from Set Pieces:Turkey Super League Application,* 2016.

Tsokaktsidis, Michail. *Coaching Transition Play.* Soccer Tutor, 2017.

Turek, Steven. *Fundamental Attacking Strategies.* Institute of Youth Soccer, 2016.

Tweedale, Alistair. *The Growing Role of Set-pieces: A Premier League Trend or a brief Aberration on our Beautiful Game?* Telegraph, August 8, 2019.

Verheijen, Raymond. *Conditioning for soccer.* Reedswain, 1998

Walker, Sam. *The Captain Class: The Hidden Force that creates the World's Greatest Teams.* Random House, 2017.

Wilson, Jonathan. *Inverting the Pyramid: A History of Football Tactics.* Orion Books, 2008.

ALSO BY TONY ENGLUND

Soccer Transition Training (with John Pascarella) (Foreword by Amos Magee)

Soccer Goalkeeper Training: The Comprehensive Guide (with John Pascarella)

Style and Domination: A Tactical Analysis of FC Barcelona (Foreword by Jeff Tipping)

Small Group Training (Foreword by Tony Sanneh)

Elite 1 vs. 1 Training (Foreword by Anson Dorrance)

Players' Roles and Responsibilities in the 4-3-3: Attacking

Players' Roles and Responsibilities in the 4-3-3: Defending

Goalie Wars

Goalie Wars Redux (e-book)

25 Activities for Training U6/U8 Players (e-book)

25 Activities for Training U6/U8 Players: Volume II (e-book)

Complete Season Curriculum for U10 (e-book)

Complete Season Curriculum for U12 (e-book)

Complete Season Curriculum for U14 (e-book)

Goalkeeper Season Curriculum (e-book)

Team-building (e-book)

ENDNOTES

[i] Tweedale, Alistair. *The Growing Role of Set-pieces: A Premier League Trend or a brief Aberration on our Beautiful Game?* Telegraph, August 8th, 2019.

[ii] Power, et al. *Mythbusting Set-Pieces in Soccer* (2018), page 1.

[iii] Power, et al. *Mythbusting Set-Pieces in Soccer* (2018), page 6.

[iv] Toplardan, Duran. *Quantitative Analysis of Goals Scored from Set Pieces:Turkey Super League Application,* 2016.

[v] Toplardan, Duran. *Quantitative Analysis of Goals Scored from Set Pieces:Turkey Super League Application,* 2016.

[vi] Tweedale, Alistair. *The Growing Role of Set-pieces: A Premier League Trend or a brief Aberration on our Beautiful Game?* Telegraph, August 8th, 2019

[vii] Pulling, Craig. *Long Corner Kicks in the English Premier League* (2015) 197-199, and Power, et al. *Mythbusting Set-Pieces in Soccer*(2018), page 1.

[viii] Tweedale, Alistair. *The Growing Role of Set-pieces: A Premier League Trend or a brief Aberration on our Beautiful Game?* Telegraph, August 8th, 2019.

[ix] Power, et al. *Mythbusting Set-Pieces in Soccer* (2018), page 1.

[x] Power, et al. *Mytbusting Set-Pieces in Soccer* (2018), page 1.

[xi] Power, et. al. *Mythbusting Set-Pieces in Soccer* (2018), page 1.

[xii] Power, et al. *Mythbusting Set-Pieces in Soccer* (2018), page 1.

[xiii] Power, et al. *Mythbusting Set-Pieces in Soccer* (2018), page 1.

[xiv] Power, et al. *Mythbusting Set-Pieces in Soccer* (2018), page 1.

[xv] Lyttleton, Ben. *Twelve Yards: The Art and Psychology of the Perfect Penalty Kick* (2014), pages 150, 171.

[xvi] Lyttleton, Ben. *Twelve Yards: The Art and Psychology of the Perfect Penalty Kick* (2014), page 169.

[xvii] Lyttleton, Ben. *Twelve Yards: The Art and Psychology of the Perfect Penalty Kick* (2014), pages 173-174.

[xviii] Lyttleton, Ben. *Twelve Yards: The Art and Psychology of the Perfect Penalty Kick* (2014), pages 170-171.

[xix] Toplardan, Duran. *Quantitative Analysis of Goals Scored from Set Pieces:Turkey Super League Application,* 2016.

Credits

Cover design: Hannah Park

Interior design: Anja Elsen

Layout: DiTech Publishing Services, www.ditechpubs.com

Cover photo: © AdobeStock

Interior diagrams: Easy Sports Graphics, sports-graphics.com

Managing editor: Elizabeth Evans

Copyeditor: Anne Rumery

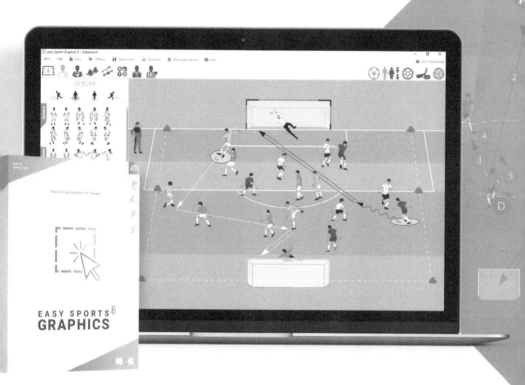

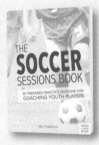

FROM MEYER & MEYER SPORT

Carl Wild

THE INTELLIGENT SOCCER COACH

PLAYER-CENTERED SESSIONS TO DEVELOP
CONFIDENT, CREATIVE PLAYERS

Gives any aspiring or experienced coach everything they need
to create the ideal environment to develop youth soccer players.

312 p., in color, Paperback, 6.5 x 9.5", ISBN: 978-1-78255-255-3, $19.95 US

Rob Ellis

THE SOCCER COACH'S TOOLKIT

MORE THAN 250 ACTIVITIES
TO INSPIRE AND CHALLENGE PLAYER

More than 250 high-quality activities for all age ranges and
playing abilities to be used in practices.

564 p., in color, Paperback, 6.5 x 9.5", ISBN: 978-1-78255-217-8, $28.95 US

Professor Miachael Gleeson

NUTRITION FOR TOP PERFORMANCE
IN SOCCER

EAT LIKE THE PROS TO TAKE
YOUR GAME TO THE NEXT LEVEL

Provides basic information on soccer sports nutrition, looking
into what elite players eat and drink.

328 p., in color, Paperback, 6.5 x 9,5", ISBN: 978-1-78255-230-7, $24.95 US

MEYER & MEYER Sport
Von-Coels-Str. 390
52080 Aachen
Germany

Phone   +49 02 41 - 9 58 10 - 13
Fax   +49 02 41 - 9 58 10 - 10
E-Mail   sales@m-m-sports.com
Website   www.m-m-sports.com

MEYER
& MEYER
SPORT